6
QUESTIONS
THAT CAN
CHANGE
YOUR LIFE

6
QUESTIONS
THAT CAN
CHANGE
YOUR LIFE

Completely.
Dramatically.
Forever.

BY JOSEPH NOWINSKI, PH.D.

RODALE

© 2002 by Joseph Nowinski, Ph.D.

Printed in the United States of America
Rodale Inc. makes every effort to use acid-free ♾, recycled paper ♲.

Interior Designer: Leanne Coppola
Cover Designer: Carol Angstadt

Library of Congress Cataloging-in-Publication Data

Nowinski, Joseph.
  6 questions that can change your life : completely, dramatically, forever / by Joseph Nowinski.
     p.   cm.
  ISBN 1–57954–557–2 hardcover
  1. Change (Psychology)   2. Change (Psychology)—Case studies.
I. Title: Six questions that can change your life.   II. Title.
  BF637.C4 N69   2002
  158.1—dc21   2002000230

Distributed to the book trade by St. Martin's Press

2 4 6 8 10 9 7 5 3 1 hardcover

RODALE

WE **INSPIRE** AND **ENABLE** PEOPLE TO IMPROVE
THEIR LIVES AND THE WORLD AROUND THEM

FOR MORE OF OUR PRODUCTS
WWW.RODALESTORE.COM
(800) 848-4735

for GREGORY

CONTENTS

ACKNOWLEDGMENTS

A book is not a one-person effort; from inception to final publication, it is a group project. I therefore want to acknowledge the contributions of several people to *6 Questions That Can Change Your Life*, beginning with my agent, Linda Konner, for her unflagging enthusiasm for the concept of the book, for her thoughtful comments on the initial proposal, and for her most able representation.

From the beginning, the team at Rodale has been generous in their support of this project. Their steady encouragement was highly motivating, and their reactions and suggestions made the book even better as it moved along. I am grateful to the many people at Rodale who took the time to read and respond to the manuscript. In particular, I want to thank editors Roz Siegel, Mariska van Aalst, and Mary South, who seemed to relate to the ideas presented here as much as I did. Finally, I want to thank Tami Booth, a true mover and shaker, for seeing the project through from start to finish.

Introduction

It isn't where you've been . . .
it's where you're going that matters in the end.

The experience of helping hundreds of people who've sought to change their lives in a positive way has taught me one important rule: Analyzing your past may be less important than discovering a vision for your future. That vision is the true starting point for dramatic, all-encompassing change—a personal transformation called *quantum change*.

6 Questions That Can Change Your Life offers you a road map for creating your own vision for the future, the imaginative leap that leads to quantum change. Like the visions of many of the people whose stories are recounted in this book, your vision may appear when you least expect it, yet it will hold the power to transform your life in extraordinary ways. In these pages, you will meet a man whose vision came to him in a dream and a woman whose vision was triggered by a passage from a children's bedtime story. You will meet a man whose vision came to him in an old photograph and a woman whose life changed course as the result of a child's question. These visions pointed out each individual's path—and then gave him or her the energy to begin the journey.

As you read, you may wonder if you're capable of having a vision or if you even need one. The answer to both of these questions is an unequivocal *yes*. Even if you've never experienced a blinding light of insight about which direction your life should take, the truth is that you're already acting according to a very specific plan. *6 Questions That Can Change Your Life* can help you determine whether that plan is truly your own or perhaps inherited from someone else.

You see, all of us go through our lives seeking answers to certain fundamental questions. These questions help us define key psychological themes for our lives, such as identity and our sense of place in the world. Guided by messages we may have heard from our parents or developed as defenses against pain and fear, we may unconsciously seek answers to the wrong questions. We look at the world as if through a set of distorted lenses—sure, we can see through them, but our perspective becomes fuzzy, muddled, confused. We may look at financial success and the accumulation of beautiful things as ends in themselves, and then feel oddly discouraged and unrewarded when we actually achieve them. We may crave excitement to break us out of our boring routines, or yearn for inner serenity and peace of mind, only to remain in our ruts and have contentment continually elude us. Searching for answers, we may create elaborate rituals or dabble in various religions, or continually rake through the remains of our childhoods for explanations or clues to our behavior. We want hints, any sign that will tell us where to go, and what we're meant to do. We find none. Feeling empty and adrift, we wonder if there truly is any point to all of this.

Of course there is. The impulse that drives us to search for meaning is valid and honorable—it is, in fact, the work of being human. But seeking answers *outside* ourselves is effort that is ultimately wasted. Visionary insight and dramatic change are possible—and we don't have to trek to a mountaintop monastery, starve ourselves, or join a cult to experience them.

As I will show you through the stories of people just like you, these *6 Questions That Can Change Your Life* will teach you how to craft a set of clean, clear lenses, custom built for you. Through these lenses, you'll view your life—your identity, your place, your purpose—with a clarity and focus that may have eluded you in the past.

Explosive energy and the capacity for quantum change already exist, right there *inside* of you. These six questions will be your guide, helping you to embrace that energy and to channel it into changing your life.

Questions, Visions, and Quantum Change: Reawakening to Your Truest Life

At age thirty-six, Stephanie, a successful Manhattan attorney, found herself adrift. Her husband of ten years had come home one day and blithely announced that he wanted a divorce. Shocked, numb, and disgusted by the idea of remaining in the home that they'd shared, Stephanie immediately handed her husband the keys to their apartment and headed out to her parents' house in Connecticut.

The city that had once seemed so warm and alive had instantly turned cold and lonely. She needed a temporary refuge to heal and feel safe. As she drove out of New York, she made a bargain with herself: *My parents' house is just a temporary landing,* she thought. *I'll only stay until I can get back on my feet, save money for a condo, and move out on my own.*

Stephanie's parents' home was spacious, so she knew her visit wouldn't be an imposition. In fact, as soon as they'd heard the news, they'd encouraged her to come. But as she drove back to her childhood home, her heart started to pound. She'd made so many strides since she'd moved to the city. Running home to Mommy and Daddy wasn't where Stephanie wanted to be, or ever imagined she would be, at that point in her life.

As nurturing as they had tried to be, her parents had always held very high standards for Stephanie. They questioned her choices of friends, clothes, hobbies, careers—gradually wearing down any efforts she made to assert herself. And now here she was, decades later, walking directly back into the same lion's den, seeking comfort and security. It seemed to Stephanie as though no place would ever feel safe. She knew something had to change. She was looking for a way out. That's when she came to see me.

QUESTIONS: READJUSTING YOUR LENSES

"My parents have always been good providers," Stephanie told me. "They're very generous with their money and their time." She paused and smiled. "But maybe they were a little too generous with their attention."

With her parents' ever-vigilant magnifying glass trained on her, ready to correct every errant step or decision, Stephanie had grown up with a feeling that she'd never be good enough for her parents. She knew her father was basically a caring person, but his perfectionism tended to spill over onto those around him. As a young girl, Stephanie developed a pitch-perfect Daddy imitation that she carried around in her head—his voice was always there with ready critique, questioning the dress she picked out for school, the colors she used in art class, even the words she spoke when talking to her best friends. Her whole life was a cacophony of "shoulds," each trumpeted into her ear by her own internalized version of her father.

Stephanie's mother offered little comfort. Her success as an attorney protected her from her husband's steady stream of criticism, but instead of helping her daughter build up her own armor, her achievements seemed only to raise the bar for her daughter's accomplishments. Stephanie had no siblings to deflect or absorb some of their attention; her closest allies were two female cousins. Slowly, between her father's constant nitpicking and her mother's monumental stature, the teenage Stephanie had faded into the woodwork. Now, the adult Stephanie feared that the same thing would happen all over again. That's when we began to work with the six questions.

Searching for Direction

Living with her parents proved every bit as difficult as Stephanie had expected. Time had taken some of the edge off her father's critical disposition, and her mother had shifted into a slower pace, but when she came to see me, Stephanie had never felt so unhappy. Despite a successful career, a good salary, and numerous friends, Stephanie still felt as though something was missing in her life.

I explained to Stephanie that all of our lives are organized and executed around the drive to answer certain elemental questions. Very likely, we inherited these questions, or ways of looking at the world, before we were experienced enough to stand up for ourselves. Reframing these questions in a new way could shed light on the ways that we've come to hide our truest selves. For Stephanie, the first of the six questions—**Who am I?**—was very different from *Who should I be?*—the one she'd answered when she originally set out on her career path. Stephanie knew who her parents thought she *should* be—an attorney—but she realized that she'd never thought about who she *was*.

The shift in the way she asked this fundamental question gave Stephanie weeks' worth of food for thought about her identity. Initially, she desperately wanted to get out of her parents' house—she thought that was the answer to all of her problems. But as she worked with the six questions, she began to realize that unless she could work out what was missing in her life, no matter where she lived—with her parents, with her husband, on her own—she would always feel lost.

As she delved into each question, Stephanie would find her thoughts shifting back and forth between the questions, as insights from one naturally fed into others. Without even realizing it, Stephanie was preparing her mind for her vision. This process of working with the questions helps us peel back the layers of years of people-pleasing and self-delusion, of disappointment, fear, and compensation, to reveal our truest inner selves.

The seed of Stephanie's breakthrough was planted when she began to ask herself the fifth question—*Who loves me?*—instead of her old question—*What am I worth?* Until then, she'd always seen herself as something of a commodity, to be valued on the basis of her position and income. "I guess I've come to think of myself as my résumé," she said, only half kidding. She'd rarely thought about how much she felt loved, either in her family or in her marriage. As a result, she'd endured a relationship in which she felt unappreciated and unloved, and she probably would've stayed in it indefinitely if her husband hadn't found someone else. It was this realization that finally triggered a visionary experience for Stephanie and led her to change her goals and the direction of her life.

Finding the Way

One Sunday, at a family birthday party, Stephanie found herself sitting on a couch, nestled between her cousin's two daughters, laughing and listening to them tell her all about their latest exploits. All of a sudden, a sense of pure comfort and ease enveloped her. She realized that, in that place and at that moment, she felt truly loved.

"I love my nieces deeply, and they love me, but it was more than that," she said. "It was like an awakening. It hit me that these children couldn't care less whether I had a husband or not, or whether I was a partner in the firm or not. They weren't the least bit interested in my résumé. They were responding to my love for them, and to our relationship. I still get a rush when I think back on that moment."

As Louis Pasteur once said, "Chance favors only the prepared mind"—we are truly ready to discover something only if we've done our homework beforehand. Using the six questions instead of a microscope, Stephanie had started to make the connections that prepared her heart and her mind to receive the new vision for her life.

VISIONS: CATALYSTS FOR CHANGE

In most people, a visionary experience like Stephanie's yields a deep sense of renewal. For her, the vision represented the opening of a door to relief and self-acceptance, to heightened energy and a new sense of direction. Still, visions can also trigger feelings of anxiety. These visions mean change, a challenge to the status quo. They may dare us to find a wellspring of courage inside. But no matter when a vision occurs, we always have the power of choice—we can choose either to pursue it or to turn and walk the other way.

Stephanie chose not to turn. Her vision proved to be pivotal in her life, initiating a domino effect of change. She said it was like being in an airplane, coming out of the clouds. After working with the six questions, and sitting with her nieces that day, she knew that what she valued most were relationships and love. From deep in her gut, she became aware that one of her goals in life was to raise a child, even if that meant adopting one. She recognized just how unhappy she had been living in the city, how little it felt like a home to her, and how difficult it had been to make close friends in the large, competitive firm she worked for. She finally admitted to herself that she deeply missed the semirural life she had known growing up, the woods and lakes she had loved as a child and teenager. In order for Stephanie to find her place in the world, she knew that she would need to look for work elsewhere, even if that meant making less money.

True to the nature of the illuminating vision, all of these ideas came together fairly quickly as a coherent plan. Stephanie began to look for work outside the city, caring not a whit about the firms' prestige. Instead of Fortune 500 clients and top-tier bonuses, she looked for reasonable work hours, warm coworkers, and the chance to do satisfying pro bono work. Although her top priority was getting settled in a new job in a new town, Stephanie decided that she'd consider dating, if the right guy came around. But she wasn't holding her breath, and she certainly wouldn't be organizing her life around him. Having turned her back on the question *What am I worth?* she was ready to experience a little "me" time, without worrying about her value to other people.

Stephanie also made an appointment at an adoption agency. In thinking about the question *Why am I here?* she'd decided that she wanted to have a child of her own, with or without a spouse. In three years, if she hadn't yet found a man who shared her values and was open to the idea of trying to conceive a child, she would go ahead on her own and adopt. She really didn't care what her parents or anyone else thought of this plan. She was resolute and determined. For perhaps the first time in her life, Stephanie was living the answers to her own questions.

Waking Up to Your Life

Have you ever had this kind of experience—an image that told you in clear and certain terms the direction that your life should take? If so, you know what a vision is. And if you've experienced this phenomenon, chances are you haven't forgotten it. True visions pack a vivid emotional punch. They don't fade easily; they endure in our memories and sometimes continue to gnaw at us even when we wish they would go away. Bill Wilson, a cofounder of Alcoholics Anonymous, described his own visionary experience as he lay in a hospital bed following yet another bout of heavy drinking.

> Suddenly the room lit up with a great white light. I was caught up into an ecstasy which there are no words to describe. It seemed to me, in the mind's eye, that I was on a mountain and that a wind not of air but of spirit was blowing. And then it burst on me that I was a free man.
>
> —from *A.A.: The Story*, by Ernest Kurtz

This experience led to Bill's quantum change, first into a sober man, then into the father of the twelve-step recovery process. Not everyone has this same kind of dramatic spiritual awakening. Visions do not necessarily involve an image of God or a burning bush. But spiritual or not, visions are powerful and unforgettable. What these moments of insight always have in common is that they show us a new direction that our lives could take if we had the courage to embrace them. They bring an awareness that we have the power of choice: that we are, indeed, free men and women.

As a rule, I've found that people tend to be both suspicious of and excited about the idea of quantum change. Even those who love you can be uncomfortable and frankly skeptical if you report having an epiphany of this kind. Also, just having a vision is no guarantee that you will go through a period of quantum change. The freedom of choice that comes with this sudden clarity turns out to be a double-edged sword. You can expect to experience anxiety along with excitement, fear along with exhilaration. You may encounter resistance from outside, as well as from within yourself. Working through these internal and external resistances, evaluating your vision, and deciding whether to move forward make up the second part of the quantum change process.

Claiming Your Vision

A young mom named Becky once told me about a vision she had while she was pushing her two young children around a crowded shopping mall in a tandem stroller.

"I was just trying to decide whether I wanted coffee or not, when all of a sudden, it came to me," she recalled. "What I really

•

wanted—without any doubt at all—was to sell our large house, which costs us a small fortune in heat and air-conditioning bills, and buy a small place in Vermont." She saw her family living within an hour's drive of her sister, who had already relocated there the year before. She could picture the house they'd live in, the school her kids would attend, even the grocery store where they would shop, with total clarity.

That night, when he came home from work, Becky told her husband about her vision. At first he was amused, but when he realized she was serious, he got angry. "He told me I was being impulsive," she said. "He started defending where we live, which was funny, because I know he's as unhappy here as I am."

Was Becky's vision a mere whim? That's what her husband thought, in part because it was his wife's vision and not his own. Becky's husband was simply (and understandably) reacting with anxiety to an idea that threatened to shake up his life.

Visionary experiences can arouse anxiety and resistance—in ourselves and in others—precisely because they are so unpredictable and because, like Becky's, they can be dramatic. Some of this concern is quite reasonable. Obviously, were she and her husband to pursue her vision, it would mean a profound change in their lifestyle. It would affect virtually every aspect of their existence, from where they worked, to where they lived, to where they found new friends. They'd have to start from square one just to find new baby-sitters. Yet, having had a true vision, Becky had foreseen all of these complications and was ready to embrace them. Energized by her clear plan, she was prepared to help walk her husband through his practical objections. Her willingness to do whatever it took is the difference between a vision and a whim.

A whim feels easy, like an escape. A vision comes together like a complex and compelling melody, whose siren call you find irresistible.

While we probably all experience visions at some time in our lives, we don't all choose to follow them, usually because of fear. We'll cover these fears and other factors that may hold you back from quantum change in the later chapter called "Living the Visionary Life." Until then, use the stories and exercises to strengthen your faith in the process, because faith is the most crucial and essential ingredient in quantum change. If you trust your vision and learn what it's trying to teach you, your life can be transformed.

Focusing on the Future

Most of us get stuck in the first place because we rely too much on the eyes in the backs of our heads. We tend to spend a lot of our time looking back, poring over our histories and childhoods, rather than looking forward, to our futures. Millions of men and women have devoted even more millions of hours to raking over their pasts—through counseling, self-help books, or self-analysis—in the hope of finding a cause for their current unhappiness. More often than not, they end their searches just as frustrated as when they began.

I'm not saying we should ignore the past. Especially in cases of abuse or trauma, it can be vital to spend some time thinking and talking about our pasts. Sometimes these harsh experiences can cause us to get stuck in key developmental moments, and revealing the emotions we've kept hidden or deeply buried in our unconscious is the only way we can be released into the present, to be available to our visions and quantum change.

Understanding our personal histories can also give us important clues as to why we may have been asking ourselves the wrong questions in the first place. As Stephanie told her story, for example, it quickly became obvious that her parents' dominant and controlling personalities had left little room for young Stephanie to discover who she was. It was much easier for her to follow the path of least resistance and become an attorney, like her mother, than it was for her to find the path that was best suited to her own interests, temperament, and goals.

Analyzing our histories has its place, but it is no substitute for a vision of our futures. The problem with scrutinizing the earlier periods of our lives is that it's so easy to get caught up in them. For years, Stephanie had been mired in an endless process of raking through past events, looking for the one true moment that would explain her lack of passion or direction. But even if she had found that defining moment—as if there would be only one!—no amount of analysis could ever change what happened. And so, naturally, at some point, her self-analysis ceased to deliver new, helpful insights and instead had become a redundant exercise that left her feeling frustrated, hopeless, and adrift.

The six questions pick up where the fruitless inspection of the past leaves off. They add a whole new dimension to the process of self-exploration and healing—the *future.*

QUANTUM CHANGE: THE ROAD TO THE FUTURE

The roots of our belief in the power of visionary experiences—and in the reality of quantum change—run deep in the human spirit. The Greeks considered those who followed their visions to be the most courageous of all mankind.

> But the bravest are surely those who have the
> clearest vision of what is before them, glory and
> danger alike, and yet notwithstanding go out to
> meet it.
>
> —Thucydides, c. 460–400 B.C.

The ancient Egyptians worshiped the phoenix, the mythological bird that rose, reborn, from its own ashes. For centuries, Native American tribes have pursued quantum change through their vision quest ritual of fasting and a period of intense isolation. Many Eastern religions use the practice of meditation toward this same end.

If you are like most people, you have habits you long to change, but you're also painfully aware of how difficult that is. In order to fully appreciate the nature and power of quantum change, it's helpful to understand the different kinds of change humans are capable of.

Incremental Change

Slow but steady progress toward a specific behavioral goal captures the essence of incremental change. Almost all of us accept the existence of incremental change, so we're not threatened by it. Nutritionists, therapists, coaches, and trainers like to help clients set a specific goal, then teach them the skills necessary to accomplish that goal, whether it be to become more assertive, communicate more effectively, get more exercise, or maintain a healthier diet. They encourage their clients to gradually try out these new skills, offering support, encouragement, and specific suggestions in the hope that the clients will eventually reach their goals in a stepwise fashion. (See the graph "Incremental Change.")

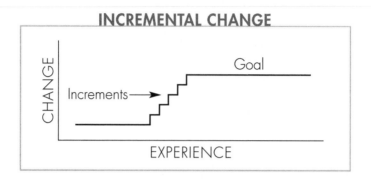

Most of us are pretty comfortable with the idea of setting a goal and then working in a slow but steady—and very predictable—way to get there. If we choose to, we can even monitor the changes we make, as in a weight-loss program, and be comforted and motivated by those small, incremental changes.

This nonthreatening kind of change is the basis of most self-help books, whether they explore weight loss or sex-life improvement. While incremental change brings comfortable, predictable progress, it can sometimes be slow and frustrating.

Still, there's absolutely nothing wrong with incremental change. In some cases, as in learning a new skill, it's essential. But many of us persevere with incremental change for years, struggling to make one small change after another in the hope that this will prove to be the road to happiness, all the while feeling frustrated and unfulfilled. These people may need something different.

Transitional Change

Transitional change is associated with passing from one stage of life to another—for instance, going from being single to joining a couple, or from being part of a couple to having a family. (See the graph "Transitional Change.")

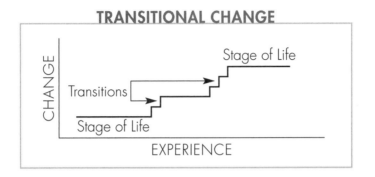

Although we can predict that most of us will pass through several stages of life (and we can even anticipate what these stages will be), the exact outcome of transitional change—the specific ways we will change as we pass from one stage of life to another—is not entirely predictable. Unlike incremental change, with its predetermined goal or outcome, transitional change doesn't give us a clear idea of where we'll be on the other end of the transition. Many singles, for example, navigate the transition to couplehood with no major crises, but their transition to parenthood may bring major problems relating to work, their social lives, or their sex lives. What turns out to be a satisfying family life for one couple may prove to be another couple's nightmare. Still, most of us are reasonably comfortable dealing with transitional changes because we can predict their arrivals as we move through life.

In some ways, transitional change overlaps with incremental change, which is why the two graphs have some similarities. Each time we pass through a developmental stage, we typically respond in an incremental way: We adjust step by step to the new situation, be it married life, parenthood, midlife, or retirement.

Even so, managing difficult transitions drives many people to seek professional help. Knowing this, most helping professionals will take a person's stage of life into account when working with her. For example, nutritionists and personal trainers know that a young woman who is pregnant with her first child needs a different approach and plan than a woman of the same age who is a college athlete and obsessed with her weight.

Quantum Change

As common as they are, incremental change and transitional change are not the only pathways open to us. Quantum change is a leap that significantly shifts the way we look at ourselves and dramatically alters the direction of our lives. This kind of change is not incremental and it is not predictable—we have no idea when it will happen or what the outcome will be. (See the graph "Quantum Change.")

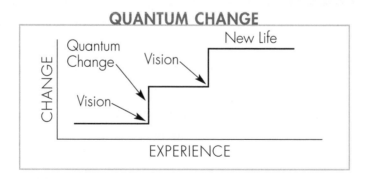

Although quantum change may be different from other forms of change, it is the way in which people have historically experienced the deepest, most significant, and most lasting shifts in their lives.

When quantum change occurs, it opens suddenly like a door before us. It's not necessarily linked with achieving any goals or developing any skills. It may or may not be associated with moving through a specific developmental stage. Instead, quantum change is a radical, sudden reorientation of the self that leads us to major decisions about lifestyles and goals. As a result, it can be unsettling. But after going through quantum change, most people tell me they sense that their actions and decisions have more meaning. They no longer have the feeling that something is missing from their lives. On the contrary, their lives become full, complete—whole.

BOB'S STORY: QUANTUM CHANGE IN ACTION

Many people spend their lives seeking the answers to the wrong questions. Consequently, the answers they come up with do not bring about the effect they're looking for—a sense of happiness, serenity, or fulfillment. These people feel as though they're walking on a treadmill, going through the motions but getting nowhere. The path they have chosen—the path they *thought* chose them—turns out to be the road to discontent, frustration, and emptiness.

Bob's experience is a great example of breaking out of that rut into fully realized quantum change. About nine months before he first came to see me, Bob had suffered a mild heart attack at the age of forty-seven. Although he'd recovered fully, the experience had obviously shaken him. His new job, the one he'd hoped would be better than his last, was also a severe disappointment. No doubt about it, Bob was seriously depressed.

Yet, as traumatic as these two major events had been, Bob felt they weren't the source of his woe. He'd been dogged by depression for as long as he could remember. He even described himself as someone who had never known what it was like to be really happy. So I could get a sense of his history, we spent one day talking about his family.

When Bob was about six years old, his parents had divorced. "Dad did work hard—but most of the time he was 'between jobs,'" Bob recalled. His dad was abusive, especially when he was out of work and on a bender. The family's address was well-known to the local police, and his father's reputation soon became contagious.

"The name Kelley was pretty much synonymous with failure," Bob said. "Whenever any of us boys got into even the slightest bit of trouble, my mother would always say that we were going to turn out to be like him. She'd say, 'It's in the blood.'"

Even after his father's death, Bob's mom continued to trash his name and accuse the boys of sharing his destiny. And as time went on, her prophecy seemed to come true. Both of Bob's brothers and four cousins on his father's side began to live the same violent, tortured lives. Only Bob escaped.

Trying to Break the Spell

In spite of the curse that hung over him like a storm cloud, Bob had managed to rise above his family's collective failure. In the twenty years since graduate school, Bob had been a social worker, climbing gradually to an administrative position of considerable responsibility—but not without personal expense. "My career probably cost me two marriages," he said.

Each marriage had produced a daughter, but the devastation wrought by the divorces, coupled with his preoccupation with work and the simple desire to avoid emotional pain, had cost Bob his relationships with both of his children. His first wife had moved out of state with no advance notice when their daughter, Marie, was barely four years old. He had tried to maintain a relationship with Marie despite the two hundred miles that separated them, but he could see her only once a month. He'd drive several hours each way, rent a motel room, and be sure to have her back by six o'clock. Constantly battling his ex-wife, Bob watched as his relationship with Marie diminished steadily over time.

Bob's daughter from his second marriage, Laura, was now in high school and devoted to school and athletics. He still had contact with her, but his relationship with her was undermined by his second ex-wife's campaign against him. According to Bob, she'd done everything she could to cast him in the role of villain. As a result, Laura kept some distance between herself and him, in loyalty to her mother.

Slowly, painfully, Bob drifted out of his daughters' lives and sought refuge in work. "I found it easier to be busy at the office," he explained. "I've always known that this is one area in which I can be consistently successful. I've never felt that way about my relationships."

One bright spot for Bob was his five-year relationship with Rose. Although they maintained separate homes, the two spent most nights and weekends together. "In my heart, I believe Rose truly loves me, more than anyone ever has," he said. "But there are times when I feel that I don't deserve it. Sometimes I think I'm just too selfish and moody to love anyone."

Seeking a New Path

When people fundamentally dislike themselves, they can be terribly critical and intolerant of those around them. It's as though their unhappiness, frustration, and self-loathing leak out onto others. For Bob, therapy, group counseling, and even antidepressants hadn't helped. Virtually every professional had told Bob that he needed to work through his history of abuse and abandonment in order to get better. To Bob, these pronouncements only meant that the old "Kelley curse" was being confirmed, this time by professionals instead of his mother or his ex-wife.

Instead of focusing on the past, Bob agreed to start working with the six questions. As he worked with each question, Bob confronted a lot of the painful issues that had kept him stuck for so long. He realized that, as far as he'd come, he still felt trapped by the Kelley curse—he felt unloving and unlovable. Each question revealed another layer of truth that Bob had sought to smother with work, trinkets, and sarcasm. But for Bob, it was the second question that had the most resonance.

What do I want?, the question that had determined his motivation for as long as he could remember, had definitely won him a house full of things. He had more material delights than he could have dreamed of as a child. Yet no amount of *stuff* could ever fill the hole his daughters had left behind. Instead of *What do I want?* Bob saw that the alternative, one of the six question—**Why am I here?**—could help him immediately zero in on the true, enduring purpose for his life, beyond the accumulation of things. Once Bob began to focus on this question, his mind became primed and ready—and his vision was soon to follow.

The Vision in the Photograph

I asked Bob to bring some old family photos to one of our talks. He showed up with a weathered-looking manila envelope containing only a few photos that nonetheless spanned nearly the length of his life.

Included in his small but rich collection of photos was one of Bob lying on his back in the grass, holding a one-year-old Marie aloft above him. Father and daughter beamed at each other with obvious love. Another photo showed Bob and Laura joyfully playing in a swimming pool. Bob gazed down at the photos for a long time. When he looked up, there were tears in his eyes.

The next time we met, Bob told me that those photos had haunted him all week. "I realized that, once upon a time, I had had a vision for my life," he said. "It was to have a normal, happy family. I could even see the house, the kids, the dog, the picket fence—the whole thing." He sighed. "Ironic, isn't it, the way things turned out—that the one thing I wanted most, I've failed at?"

Failure is a very harsh word that's ill-suited to affairs of the heart. We may stumble or lose our way, but there is rarely a moment at which we cannot come back and reclaim what's missing. Was it reasonable to expect that Bob should actually start over and build another family? Probably not. The best, most healing thing Bob could do was try to build on what was there: He'd have to reach out to his daughters, wherever they were, and hope that they would reach back.

Despite his understandable fear of rejection and his doubts about his ability to love, Bob decided that the risks were worth the potential payoff—he would have some semblance of a happy family, with or without the picket fence. He decided to bond with Laura by showing up at her athletic events, in spite of the risk of bumping into his ex-wife. He started coming to more of her games, waving to her from the stands, cheering his heart out along with the other parents. When he'd start to get nervous, he'd just cheer louder, and once he got over his initial anxiety, he had a great time. His investments of time and cheering paid off—one day, after the final whistle, Laura bounded over to her dad and suggested that they get together for breakfast some Sunday morning. A new relationship was born.

The Hardest Challenge

Bob's second challenge was much harder: to attempt to track down his older daughter, Marie. He knew that Marie might not want to have anything to do with him, considering that they hadn't spoken in ten years. When she was fourteen, her mother had moved a second time, leaving no forwarding address. Bob harbored a great deal of guilt and sadness over not doing his best to pursue the issue further during all the intervening years.

He was sure his absence had hurt Marie, and he was terrified of hurting her again. But the photo he'd found had reminded Bob of the close relationship they'd once shared. Bob decided it was better to take the risk and reach out. Even if she ended up saying "No, thanks," at least he would know that he'd tried.

I didn't hear from Bob again for more than two months. When he called, I almost didn't recognize his voice on my answering machine—his message was full of energy and smiles. Later that week, a changed man walked into my office. Bob looked younger—much younger—than the man I'd shaken hands with at the end of our last session. He stood upright and looked me right in the eye. The Bob I'd come to know had permanent lines of stress (or had it been sadness?) etched into his forehead. Not so the man who sat across from me now, telling me the story of how he had found Marie.

Vision into Action

Stored away in one of the many boxes that cluttered his attic, Bob had found Marie's birth certificate with her Social Security number. Thanks to the Internet, this was all the information he needed to be able to locate her. She was living in a semirural area of Pennsylvania, about a four-hour drive from his home.

After he'd located her, Bob walked around with Marie's address and phone number in his wallet for nearly a month before he made another move. He wrote and rewrote a letter to her countless times. Once, he pulled his letter back just as he was about to drop it into a mailbox.

The note he finally sent was short, gentle, and direct. He took full responsibility and apologized to Marie for losing contact with her. He acknowledged that he could have made more of an effort to find her when her mother had moved. The truth was, he wrote, it had been too painful to him to contemplate a long-distance relationship in which he might only get to see Marie once in a while, if at all. As time passed, it became more and more awkward to think about contacting her. He deeply regretted the path he had chosen.

Bob told Marie that he loved her very much and hoped that she was well and happy. He said he would welcome any contact that she might agree to, but also said he would understand if she was angry or hurt and preferred to be left alone. He ended the note by promising that he would not write again if Marie chose not to contact him. He sent it via certified mail.

Bob showed me the letter he'd received in return from Marie. It too had been sent by certified mail. It was written in a small, neat hand. Like his, it was brief and to the point:

> Dear Dad,
> Thanks for the apology. I definitely appreciate it. For a long time I thought maybe it was my fault that we lost contact. Anyway, the answer is *yes*, I *would* like to talk to you, and to *see* you sometime if possible. You're right, there is some pain and anger on my end. But I have to admit that I respect you for having the courage to find me and write, even after all this time. Since you now know how to reach me, please call or write soon.
> Love,
> Marie
> P.S.: Don't wait so long this time! Life is too short.

By taking the time to work through the six questions, Bob had readied his mind to receive his vision. When he took that photo in his hand, he was open and able to accept that simple and striking intuition that told him where he needed to go.

Granted, he still wasn't perfect—not by a long shot. Bob had major work to do on his relationships and his addiction to work. On the other hand, he no longer felt lost. The depression that had dogged him since childhood was lifting. He was happier, more at peace with himself, and this in turn influenced his outlook on the future. His work relationships had become less of a struggle and more of a pleasure. "You can even catch me smiling around the office now," he admitted.

His girlfriend, Rose, had noticed the change in him, too. She confessed that as much as she had liked Bob, she had doubted she could ever live with him—until now.

Bob's vision wasn't new—in fact, he'd had it for years. But when Bob had changed his main question from *What do I want?* to ***Why am I here?*** the openness that had come from doing the work and asking himself the six questions gave him the courage to embrace his vision rather than turn away. Invigorated with a sense of new possibility, Bob was now solidly on the path to quantum change.

Are you ready to take the first step to quantum change? Let's look more closely at the first, most fundamental of the six questions: ***Who am I?***

FIRST QUESTION:

Who Am I?

vs.

Who Should I Be?

MEELY FOUND
HER TRUE SELF

Early on, Meely showed a passion for speed and adventure. When she was seven, she and her sister built a homemade roller coaster out of several planks and a lard-greased wooden box. When she launched herself from the top of an eight-foot toolshed, she quickly slammed into a trestle and tore her dress. Undaunted, she was thrilled and thirsted for more.

Born at the turn of the twentieth century, Meely grew up attending private schools and enjoying many of the privileges of her grandparents' wealth. Despite their love for Meely and her sister, her grandparents were not fans of her father, a creative, flighty spendthrift who told fantastical stories and just barely managed to keep his family from slipping into poverty.

When Meely's father's troubles worsened, she and her sister were often left with relatives or friends while her parents tried to regroup. Frustrated, her father turned to drink, and soon his family's leading position in society was tarnished by petty gossip and pitying looks.

Meely was often cast as her parents' go-between, forced to buttress their failing relationship, and consequently she developed a sense of responsibility for the well-being of others. After seeing firsthand the suffering of World War I veterans, she enrolled in pre-med at Columbia University. She studied hard and showed great promise, but a doctor's life just didn't feel quite right to her. When another bout of her father's drinking called her back to California at age twenty-three, she left school willingly—though with no idea what she wanted to do with her life.

That year, at an aerial meet in Long Beach, she was handed a helmet and glasses so she could board the open-cockpit biplane for a ten-minute flight over Los Angeles. The pilot requested that another man be on board in case the "nervous lady" decided to jump overboard. He needn't have worried—as soon as the plane left the ground, she knew she had to learn how to fly . . . and that's how pilot Amelia Earhart found her wings.

Who Am I?

The basis for our entire relationship with the world begins with a simple understanding of how we can get what we need, and this understanding starts to develop the second we're born. As babies and small children, we learn the rules pretty quickly: Cry and get food and comfort. Smile and say "Pretty please!" and be rewarded with a hug and maybe a toy we've had an eye on.

If the rules stopped developing right there, not one of us would ever have a problem getting our needs met. But these rules became ever more complicated as we grew older. A smile once may have gotten us off the hook, but as teens and adults we had to decode an intricate system of expectations and obedience to gain approval. (Try crying to get your next promotion and see how well it works!) The sooner we mastered the new rules, the more benefits—the pat on the back, the use of Dad's car, the bigger sales bonus—we were afforded.

Ah, and therein lies the rub. To get what we wanted—praise and respect—we had to abide by the rules; but those same rules were put in place to keep us from constantly grabbing at our most basic desires. We strove to be good girls and boys, we tried to be praised and accepted, and, over time, we turned our backs on our truest selves in the process.

FRAGMENTATION VERSUS WHOLENESS

The Catch-22 of growing up affects us all to varying degrees—some of us, with the help of encouraging parents and a supportive environment, can strike a balance between others' expectations and our own desires. However, most of us struggle for a long time trying to carve out a clear sense of who we are. That's why our first question tackles the question of identity. Rather than ask ourselves *Who should I be?*—a question designed to lead us *outside* ourselves—we can ask ourselves *Who am I?*—a question that focuses on looking *inside* for the answers.

The question *Who am I?* invites us to explore our temperaments, our tastes, and our talents, leading us toward a sense of personal integration, wholeness, and self-acceptance. When we allow ourselves to ask this question, we're building a solid foundation of resilient self-esteem that can help us to discover a vision for our lives. In contrast, focusing on the question *Who should I be?* creates a sense of fragmentation. Based entirely on looking to others to define ourselves, this approach to life and identity leads to confusion, anxiety, and fragile self-esteem.

Many of us spend our formative years developing an identity based on *Who should I be?* We attempt to live up to an amalgam of messages from our families, our peers, and society. Their expectations collect into an ideal image that we try to re-create, only dimly aware that the image originates outside of ourselves.

These external forces are almost impossible to resist. For example, the need to be successful, financially and otherwise, is constantly reinforced by those close to us and by the culture at large. Regardless of how well-intentioned our parents might have been, there is a definite risk involved in yielding to their expectations without giving conscious thought to what is being sacrificed.

Take Celia's story. Her parents sat her down during her junior year of high school and told her they'd be willing to pay for her college education, as long as she studied education or nursing. If she wanted to study something else—anything else—she would have to pay her own way.

When she looks back, Celia genuinely believes that her parents thought they were acting in her best interests. But despite their good intentions, they were asking the wrong question: *Who should Celia be?* Instead, they could have encouraged Celia to ask herself **Who am I?** and then stepped back and had faith in her ability to find her own path.

Despite the fact that she yielded to her parents, Celia had one advantage many others don't: Her parents were frank about their expectations. In most cases, we yield to expectations that remain unconscious, buried in the back of our minds, because the people who were trying to shape us weren't very open about their plans for us. But when we let family, friends, or society decide who we should be, we risk nothing less than our entire lives. We eventually find ourselves wandering on a path we didn't choose, living someone else's life instead of our own. Pursuing someone else's vision of the good life demands that you spend a lot of time talking yourself into making it your own. Many people, like Sally, have done exactly that.

SALLY'S STORY: HER FATHER'S DAUGHTER

Sometimes it takes a reminder of our own mortality to shock us into examining the lives we've chosen. Such was the case with

Sally. Two years before we met, when she was thirty-eight, she had been diagnosed with an ovarian tumor, the same condition that had claimed the life of her grandmother and nearly took her mom.

Initially, the fact that surgery would cut her fertility in half didn't faze her—she just wanted the thing out of her body. Gradually, though, as the day of her surgery approached, a growing dread began to press on her. Although she and her husband, Greg, hadn't made a conscious decision to start a family, they also hadn't ruled it out. But then her doctor said that the combination of her age and the removal of one ovary could make it difficult for her to get pregnant even if she wanted to. Sally had never considered the possibility of not being able to have kids, and she was rattled in a way she'd never been before.

Thanks to early detection, the surgery and aggressive treatment were effective. Sally's tumor was removed, analyzed, and found to be benign. Her medical prognosis was good.

Throughout her ordeal, Greg continued to be supportive and loving, strong without being overbearing. "He's so different from my first husband," said Sally. "My ex was an immature party boy who wanted me to support him for the rest of his life, but Greg really carries his share of the load."

Sally saw Greg as a true life partner, her best friend. With his support unwavering, their love grew richer through her medical crisis—but her personal crisis was just beginning.

Relapse

About ten years before her surgery, Sally had experienced something like a vision when she walked into an Alcoholics Anonymous meeting. Convinced that *she* didn't have a problem, she nonetheless recognized that alcoholism ran in her family and she didn't want to wind up like her brothers, drunk and irresponsible. Those meetings helped Sally to realize that maybe she did have a greater problem than she realized. Alcohol had been starting to control her decisions and she resolved to remove it from her life.

She also discovered that she *liked* being around sober people. Contrary to her experiences with partying friends, Sally connected with her AA friends on a deeper level. Feeling stronger and more in control, Sally met Greg about a year later. Shortly thereafter, they fell in love, and she married for the second time.

Nine years later, about a year after her surgery, Sally started drifting away from AA. She had made a habit of attending a meeting once a week or so, but she cut back to once a month, then once every two months. When she started buying wine again, she stopped going altogether.

Initially, she would just take a few sips before throwing away the bottle. She never wanted Greg to find out and took great pains to hide her drinking from him. But then her friends from AA started calling and leaving messages, wondering how she was doing. Greg was often the first one home from work, so he heard these messages before she had a chance to erase them. When he asked her if everything was okay, she brushed him off. "I just need a little break from AA, that's all," she said. He bit his lip and tried not to worry.

When those few sips turned into gulps, Sally bottomed out suddenly and swiftly. There was no way she could hide it from Greg or her friends. One evening, Greg came home late from work and found her passed out on the couch, several empty bottles of wine on the coffee table beside her. He called one of Sally's AA friends, who came right over, sobered Sally up, and whisked her off to a meeting.

Once again, AA had helped Sally pull herself up from the lowest point. When we met, she was sober again, and going to two or three meetings a week. She had a sponsor and was back in touch with her AA friends. Her relationship with Greg had not been seriously damaged by the relapse, although it had made both of them realize that her addiction was something they needed to take seriously—they could no longer allow themselves the luxury of complacency.

Yet for all of this good progress, Sally was still horribly depressed. She readily admitted that her close encounter with the fear of cancer and infertility had shaken her. But to her, those events alone were still not enough to account for her relapse or her depression. Nothing she'd tried up to that point had really gotten to the root of her problem. That's when she began working with the six questions.

Open to Vision

Sally was off to a great start because she had faith in the concepts of visions and quantum change. She had experienced a similar epiphany the day she entered her first AA meeting, which dramatically shifted the course of her life. Now, working with the six questions taught her to approach her heartache in a totally new way. Suddenly, instead of working the twelve steps and admitting that she was powerless over her addiction, she was shifting her attention to where her true power came from—her own identity.

Although AA had no doubt saved her from the fate of her brothers—both of whom were heavy drinkers tortured by troubled relationships, problems with their children, and health maladies—Sally felt that it hadn't really changed her basic view of herself. Sobriety had made it possible for her to have a successful career and to choose a good partner, but she still struggled with the low self-esteem that had plagued her since childhood.

True to her determined character, Sally had worked hard to resolve her low self-worth—she had spent countless hours thinking about it, reading about it, talking with a counselor, taking antidepressants. In the end, she felt no better. Deeply unhappy and frustrated, she had resigned herself to living with it, until her medical crisis and her subsequent relapse sent her into a tailspin. That's when she came to me and learned that what matters most is not the questions you've been asking yourself until now—it's your willingness to try asking yourself some new ones.

Sally had two challenges ahead of her: First, she needed to shift her focus from the past to the future. Second, she needed to begin looking inward to find herself. As Sally began to work with the first question—*Who am I?*—she spent a lot of time thinking about how her development as a person had been dictated by the original question, *Who should I be?* That person, it turned out, was a perfect embodiment of all of her father's hopes and dreams. Sally was the very good girl who had forgotten how to be herself.

The Family Business

Sally's father had always been an ambitious and hardworking man. He and his brother started a painting business while in their early twenties, and soon they expanded to handyman jobs. News of their good work spread, and the business grew quickly. By the time Sally was a teen, it had become a major construction firm. Just about every person in Sally's family, male and female, made a living as a plumber, carpenter, electrician, bookkeeper, secretary, or estimator there.

Had things been different, Sally suspects that her father would have happily turned his business over to Sally's brothers. But both boys had built reputations for being wild and irresponsible, and later their drinking problems became obvious to everyone. Meanwhile, Sally enjoyed nothing better than hanging out at construction sites with her father, who gladly took her under his wing. By age twelve, Sally knew the basics of framing, Sheetrocking, plumbing, and wiring. She could even lay a clean row of bricks. In high school, she learned how to estimate projects and apply for permits. Sally had a great head for the business, and she basked in her dad's praise, never realizing that she was being groomed for a leadership role.

For as long as she could remember, Sally had been a sensitive, creative person who loved to read and write. Her family was aware of this, too, but they poked fun and teased her about it. "They said I lived with my head in the clouds," Sally said. "I tried to laugh it off, but deep down, their attitude really bugged me."

Sally was the only one in her family to go to college. Her mother seemed genuinely proud of this accomplishment, but no one else showed any interest from the day she began classes until the day she graduated. She was so embarrassed by her secret passion for writing that when she had short stories published in the college literary magazine, she didn't bother to tell anyone.

Sally spent her summers working for her father, getting to know all the management aspects of the business. Even though he never said it, she knew he'd be perfectly happy if she announced that she was quitting school to stay with the business full time. Every August, when it was time for her to return to college, Sally's father's disappointment was obvious. Every year, it became harder and harder for Sally to retain her own vision for her life.

In her heart, Sally was a teacher. What she wanted most was to pursue a master's degree, and maybe even a doctorate, in literature. She dreamed of spending her life surrounded by words and inquisitive minds. But with each passing year, her family's resistance to her true interest, combined with their constant pressure on her to take a larger role in the business, took its toll. "I remember my dad saying, more than once, that teaching was for people who couldn't make a 'real' living," Sally recalled. "Part of me wrote off these comments as ignorance—but another part of me desperately wanted his approval, and I knew that there was only one way to get it." The very day she graduated from college, her father offered her a lucrative job overseeing a major new construction project. She took it—and twenty years later, she was the depressed, unfulfilled CEO of a thriving family business.

Breakthrough

The entire weight of Sally's family, including the esteem she sought from her father, had been thrown in the direction of who they thought she *should* be. No family members had being willing to align themselves with Sally's inner spirit—and the truth was, the family had gained a great deal when Sally, competent and hardworking as she was, accepted the reins of corporate leadership. It was a feat for her to have finished college at all, considering the resistance she'd encountered.

Over the course of several months, Sally asked herself all six questions. While most people find all the questions helpful, one usually resonates most strongly. For Sally, that one was **Who am I?**

During one of our talks, we stumbled on an interesting philosophical dilemma: Did grown-up Sally see herself as a builder who could also write a good short story, or as a writer who could also build a house? Sally wanted to say "Both!" but knew she couldn't—she would have to make a choice. This choice was at the heart of **Who am I?**

When her vision came to her, Sally's experience of it was very different from her AA epiphany. She described this new vision as a deeper, more profound shift in the way she saw herself and her life. Afterward, she felt invigorated and excited for the first time in many years. As it turned out, a question akin to **Who am I?**—posed by a teenager—triggered Sally's discovery of the direction her life would take.

Several months earlier, Sally had received a call from a friend who taught in a local technical high school, to see if she'd be willing to talk to his class about the construction business. She was interested, but at first, Sally put her friend off. Finally, he called and said that if Sally couldn't fit the visit in sometime in the next two weeks, it would be too late—the school year would be over. She agreed to come in the following week.

"When I arrived at the school that morning, my uneasiness felt like a knot in my stomach," she recalled. "I tried to calm down. I told myself it wasn't like I had to give a lecture—I just had to talk about what I did for a living!" Then, as she walked into the classroom, Sally started to feel much better. The kids were nice and polite—and so *young*, she thought. She could clearly see herself at their age, when she'd first thought about becoming a teacher, when she'd first started writing stories. Then one young man raised his hand and asked a very simple question: "How did you choose your career?"

His question hit Sally like a fist. "First, I had a sudden strong urge to blurt out that I hadn't *chosen* my career at all, but more or less fell into it," she remembered. "But what really stuck with me was the thought that if this boy were my son, what advice would I give him for choosing how to spend the rest of *his* life?"

Sally's life changed in that classroom. All the work she had done with the six questions had readied her mind for one remarkable moment of clarity. There was nothing fuzzy or ambiguous about it—she felt it right down to the center of her being. As she spoke to the class, Sally realized she had three new goals for her life: to find a way to teach, to start writing again, and to talk with Greg about starting a family of their own.

Fitting the Pieces Together

In addition to providing clarity, experiences like the one Sally had are coherent. The formerly frustrating puzzle pieces of our lives suddenly all fit together. In Sally's case, she realized that she didn't have to abandon her career or quit the company to fulfill her dreams, but she would have to shift her priorities dramatically.

She came up with one easy solution we could all use—she would get more help. A couple of assistants could easily relieve some of the day-to-day responsibilities of managing the business. While hiring a few assistants would translate to less profit for the family, Sally saw that it would also give her the freedom to pursue her vision.

At the same time, Sally's friend guided her through the process of getting a teaching certificate so she could teach part time in the vocational high school. Another contact led to an opportunity to write a monthly column in a local newspaper on the subject of home improvements. "It's not exactly writing the great American novel," Sally quipped, "but at least I'll be putting pen to paper again."

Greg was delighted that Sally wanted to consult an infertility specialist and look into adoption. He told her he'd been hoping for a long time to hear such happiness in her voice and to see it in her face. The undercurrent of sadness that had been with her for so long had suddenly disappeared.

"There's always been this discontent in me on some level," Sally said. "For a time, I thought I'd grow out of it or just live with it. But now, suddenly, it's just gone." She didn't know where this path would eventually lead her, but for the first time, she knew she was heading in the right direction.

Her deepest wish was that she and Greg would one day have a child whom they could encourage to be his or her own person. Having faced up to the truth about herself, she wanted to share that freedom and delight with her own child. She knew now the wisdom of Polonius's advice to his son in *Hamlet.*

> This above all: to thine own self be true,
> And it must follow, as the night the day,
> Thou canst not then be false to any man.

REDISCOVERING WHO YOU ARE

Like the shy person urged to be more outgoing or the craftsman driven to computer programming because "That's where the jobs are," Sally had been coaxed into leading someone else's idea of the "right" life. We often make important decisions, such as how we'll spend forty hours a week for thirty or forty years, on the basis of answering the question *Who should I be?* The result? Countless numbers of us end up just going through the motions, living lives that don't really suit our true natures, wondering, "Is this all there is?"

It's surprisingly easy to lose sight, as time passes, of the person you really are—the person who lives in your heart. We are each born with a unique set of temperaments, talents, and preferences. As any parent who's had more than one child can tell you, these differences are apparent virtually from birth. They are the essence of our core personalities.

This core personality is not immutable, however. On the contrary, the second a baby is born, it is immediately exposed to many external influences: the parents rewarding smiles with smiles, the jealous sibling who secretly bullies, the baby-sitter who blows up over spilled milk. As the child's core personality interacts with varied family and social environments, his adult personality is shaped. One tragic example is people who are born with sensitive dispositions and are then exposed to abuse, chaos, or rejection. Most of these tender-hearted people are likely to develop into insecure and fearful adults instead of fulfilling their intuitive and creative potential. But if children are raised in an environment that allows them to pursue their natural talents and interests, they naturally gravitate toward those resources and activities that best fit their core personalities.

Rediscovering Your Core

Getting in touch with your core personality is not as easy as it may sound. If you simply ask yourself to describe your core personality, you may hear a lot of voices, some that may have *told* you what you are really like instead of asking you.

Use the following exercises to help pose those questions, dig into your memory, and gain insight into your true self. First, grab a journal or notebook with at least fifty pages to keep all your completed exercises and musings about the six questions in one place. Set aside fifteen to twenty minutes for each exercise, but feel free to return to them again and again, to add, refine, or tinker. As with visions, smaller insights often come to us when we'ı thinking about them.

The personality grid can help you get in touch with the "you" you were born with and detail how that essential personality was influenced by experience. Copy the blank personality grid below into your notebook and then follow the instructions.

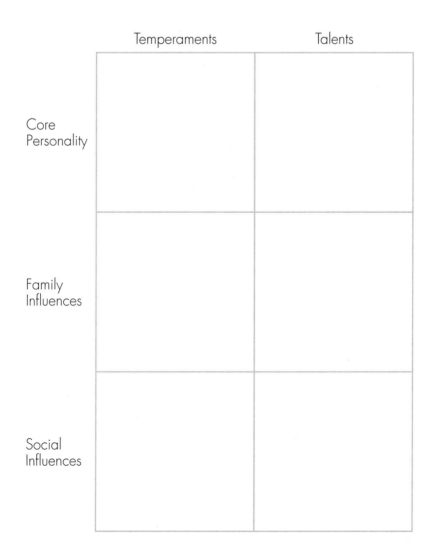

	Temperaments	Talents
Core Personality		
Family Influences		
Social Influences		

Step One: Your Temperaments

Your personality grid begins with an inventory of the key temperaments of your character, then expands to include family and social influences. The treasure you're trying to mine here springs directly from your earliest memories, so it may be helpful to tap siblings, parents, or other relatives for recollections of your childhood that can help jog your memory. But don't get bogged down with their opinions—trust your gut. If it rings true to you, write it down in the Temperaments box to the right of Core Personality.

Listed below are seven areas in which people's temperaments can differ. Some of these dimensions may overlap with one another. For each one, try to place yourself, as you believe you *naturally* are, somewhere between the two extremes that are described, and write the corresponding word into the Core Personality–Temperaments box.

Would you describe yourself as a person who is outgoing and extroverted, or would you say that you tend to be shy and introverted?

Introverted_____|_____Extroverted

Guideline: As a child, did you tend to be a natural "people person," or were you someone who preferred spending time alone? When left to your own devices, did you seek out others or did you relish your private time? (Keep in mind that most of us are not necessarily either extroverts or introverts. When used as labels, these words pigeonhole and stereotype us. In truth, we lie somewhere between these two extremes, but they're helpful for getting a brief sketch of our original core personality.)

Would you describe yourself as someone whose nature it is to be cautious, and who likes stability, or are you someone who is drawn to excitement and risk-taking?

Caution_____|_____Risk-Taking

Guideline: As a child, did you find roller coasters, climbing on rocks, and downhill skiing exciting? Or did these activities simply provoke anxiety for you? While some people seem to be born risk-takers, others prefer stability and are more comfortable with a cautious, methodical approach to life. Where on this continuum does your core personality fall?

Are you a confrontational person who is comfortable taking an aggressive stance, or are you a basically nonconfrontational person who finds it difficult and uncomfortable to be aggressive?

Confrontational_____|_____Nonconfrontational

Guideline: Mothers can often attest to differences among their children in terms of innate aggressiveness. As a child, did you find yourself involved in, or even starting, squabbles very often? Or did you occasionally find yourself the target of schoolyard taunting or bullying? Just as some of us seem to be natural risk-takers, some are born with an inclination to be aggressive and confrontational. Others can recall that they've always been nervous around or unsettled by aggression and avoid it whenever possible. Where along this continuum would you place your natural inclinations?

After a crisis or disappointment, do you tend to bounce back quickly and resiliently, or are you more sensitive, experiencing lingering aftereffects?

Resilient_____|_____Sensitive

Guideline: At one extreme on this dimension lie people who seem to be bulletproof—they easily adapt to change and are very difficult to offend or hurt. At the other extreme are people who do not cope well with change and whose feelings are easily hurt, but tend to be very empathetic and compassionate toward others. These differences in temperament are also usually apparent from an early age. Where would you place yourself on this line?

What do you like to do most in your free time: to be involved in strenuous physical activity, like running, hiking, craft work, or furniture building, or to pursue more intellectual activities, like reading, writing, or surfing the Internet?

Physical_____|_____Intellectual

Guideline: This dimension does not refer to the difference between brains and brawn. It has nothing to do with intelligence, since many people who are quite intelligent are naturally drawn to physical activity more than they are to intellectual activity. Rather, it refers to our inherent preference: Some people prefer to spend their free time growing a garden or building furniture rather than playing chess or working at their computer. Where do you think your temperament falls on this continuum?

Are you someone who prefers to plan and prepare in advance for things, or are you someone who prefers to do things on the spur of the moment?

Planner_____|_____Spontaneous

Guideline: Can you remember being comfortable with erratic schedules as a child, or did you crave routine and ritual? Some people prefer to start out on a vacation with nothing more than a destination in mind; others want a detailed itinerary, complete with maps and hotel reservations, worked out beforehand. Each of these temperamental types has its advantages and disadvantages. Most importantly, each of these temperaments is better suited to certain lifestyles. Where does your core personality fall?

Would you characterize your thinking as linear, moving from the beginning to the end of a thought in logical steps, or are you a random thinker, moving in several ways at once?

Random_____|_____Linear

Guideline: Random thinkers can often make connections and have insights that others miss. They have a high tolerance for chaos—however, their lives also tend to be a bit chaotic. They have a hard time with deadlines and they typically get bored with conventional jobs. In contrast, linear thinkers find chaos distinctly aversive and immediately try to bring order to it. Their lives tend to be organized, and they are highly reliable. Whereas linear thinkers respond emotionally to representational art, random thinkers tend to prefer abstract art.

While these seven dimensions do not even come close to an exhaustive list of human temperaments, exploring and charting them can give you a useful baseline in establishing what was once your core personality. After you've filled in the Core Personality–Temperaments box of your personality grid, turn your attention to the bottom two-thirds of the grid, where you will record the influence that family and social environment have had on your temperament.

We're often born with one distinct temperament, only to be pressured to change it. For example, quite a few men and women who were born with sensitive, intellectual natures were given the message—by family, friends, or both—that they'd be better off "toughening up," being someone other than who they were. Sally is a good example of this—no one ever encouraged her to pursue the sensitive, intellectual side of her personality. Because of children's amazing adaptability and eagerness to please, many children instinctively attempt to change their core personalities to gain approval. The fortunate child has parents who recognize and respect their child's innate disposition and strive to find friends who also support it.

Use the following questions to retrace the subtle (and not-so-subtle) influence your family may have exerted on your core personality. Write the answers in the Family Influences–Temperaments box.

- When your parents were praising you, which words did they use or which of your behaviors did they support? For example, many women can remember being praised for being pretty or well-behaved, when perhaps their true natures were to be outgoing, boisterous, and lively. What words of ultimate praise from your parents do you remember hearing?

- In which situations would your parents scold you? What words would they use? Some people remember hearing words like "lazy," "selfish," or "slow." (Hint: These are probably the words you use to chastise your adult self when you are feeling underconfident or disappointed in your performance.)

Now, to complete the Temperaments column of the personality grid, think about the messages you received about yourself from the social environment. These could include things you heard from coaches, teachers, close friends, baby-sitters, even bosses—people whom you've looked to for guidance or approval. Write the answers to these questions in the Social Influences–Temperaments box.

- When these authority figures and trusted friends complimented you, which words did they use? Did they say you were dedicated, loyal, or hardworking, or that you were "perfect" at something? Sometimes words like these, while positive, can make us believe performing for and pleasing other people is more important than listening to our own instincts. Picture each of these people smiling and write down the first word that you see coming out of their mouths.

- When these same people sought to correct you or critique you, which words did they use? Some people heard words like "crybaby" or "slacker." Picture each person scowling at you and write down the word you think he's saying.

- At this point, you're halfway done with your personality grid, which could look something like the one below.

	Temperaments	Talents
Core Personality	introverted risk-taking confrontational sensitive intellectual spontaneous random thinker	
Family Influences	focused dedicated lazy proud moody restless	
Social Influences	quiet opinionated crybaby smart	

Step Two: Your Talents

Now you're ready to fill out the right half of the personality grid, the column that charts your talents. As with our temperaments, each of us is born with a unique set of gifts that we can either pursue and develop or avoid entirely. The choice we make depends in part on the opportunities that come our way. While some children are blessed with environments that support and encourage their gifts, others are raised in a way that does not allow them to embrace their natural talents.

Our innate talents generally exist in three broad domains: intellectual, physical, and creative talents. Sally's talents extended across all three domains: She could manage complex construction projects, build houses with her bare hands, and write beautiful, imaginative stories. (How unfortunate that the talents she was pressured to ignore were those closest to her sense of who she truly was!)

When doing this exercise, many people uncover talents that they had not even thought about for years. Use the following questions to identify the talents and potentials you were born with, and write the answers in the Core Personality–Talents box.

- For three minutes, write down words that describe the talents you've had for as long as you can remember: Can you remember people's birthdays? Can you pound nails with one stroke? Can you call a tune in five notes or less? Can you imitate your brother's laugh? Write the things you are secretly most proud of.

- Try to remember your elementary-school experience. What did you like best about going to school? What were your favorite subjects?

- What did you want to be when you grew up?

- When you were alone, what did you spend the most time doing?

  Building things

  Drawing

  Writing

  Running or jumping outside

  Fixing things

  Growing plants

  Singing or dancing

  Playing with science projects, like ant farms or chemistry sets

Next, try to tease out any influence you may have received from your family. Write the answers to these questions in the Family Influences–Talents box.

Very
Impt

- What did your parents tell you would happen when you were an adult? Try to remember how they would have finished this sentence: "When you grow up, you're going to be a. . . . " Many children hear messages like "successful lawyer" or "doctor" from a tender age. (Perhaps you even heard that you'd be "president"!)

- How did your parents react when you told them what you wanted to study in school or do for extracurricular activities? Were they supportive of your desires, or did they try to encourage you to take other classes or sign up for different programs? What alternative suggestions did they make?

Finally, consider the influence you may have gotten from friends, teachers, coaches, or bosses who could have been trying to subtly guide your future—usually with the best of intentions. Write these answers in the Social Influences–Talents box.

- Do you remember ever being encouraged by your teachers to pursue any specific interests or talents as a child or adolescent? What were they? Write them down, regardless of whether or not you derived pleasure or satisfaction from them.

- Which track were you placed on in high school—technical, professional, or college prep? Did you enjoy those classes, or did you always feel like you were out of place? What words would describe the reasons others positioned you on that track? (Maybe "handy," "career minded," or "academically gifted"?)

- Have you ever accepted a promotion or a job change because the opportunity presented itself, when you weren't entirely sure it was a good fit for you? What particular assets did your boss say she was looking for when she offered you the job?

Your completed personality grid should look something like the one shown on page 56. This one chart gives you a comprehensive personal history of how your core personality was shaped into the individual you are today. When the lucky among us scan from the top row down, they see that most of the squares look very similar. However, the majority of us will see differences, sometimes even drastic ones.

	Temperaments	Talents
Core Personality	introverted risk-taking confrontational sensitive Intellectual spontaneous random thinker	good listener good memory for faces creative writing drama- putting on plays
Family Influences	focused dedicated lazy proud moody restless	science/math sports writing
Social Influences	quiet opinionated crybaby smart	good with people attentive to detail creative

Because the first question—*Who am I?*—is so central to the other five questions, the personality grid will act as a kind of index for your journey. As you work through the remainder of the six questions, if you find yourself getting stuck, flip back to the grid and focus your attention on the words next to Core Personality.

Keep thinking about those words—those temperaments and talents hold the key to your vision.

Your Autobiographical Sketch

Another exercise that can help jog your thinking and put you in touch with your core personality is writing an autobiographical sketch. The following questions will also trace the development of your core personality from childhood to adulthood. Turn to a fresh page in your journal, and as you go through the questions, write down the details from each section that seem the most meaningful to you. (Maybe you'll even want to expand on your answers from some of the questions in steps one and two from the personality grid.) These details can be useful reference points for evaluating the life you are living today. You can see how it evolved from the way you lived as a child, so much closer to your true character and interests. You'll have an opportunity to pull all of this information together in an exercise in the chapter that deals with the sixth question, *How can I be true to myself?* That's when you'll commit your answers to the six questions to paper.

If, as you write, you feel a stab of recognition—perhaps something you hadn't thought of in a long time—make sure to circle that detail and keep it in mind as you move through the six questions. Chances are, those memories will keep resurfacing as you get closer to your vision.

When you were a child . . .

- What were your favorite free-time activities?
- Did you like or dislike rough-and-tumble play?

- Did you like spending time alone? What would you do?

- Did you like spending time with others? What would you do?

- If we were to ask your parents to describe your personality as a child, what do you think they would say?

- What kinds of children did you like to hang out with, and what kinds of children did you prefer to avoid?

- In general, do you prefer physical activity over reading, or vice versa?

- What were your favorite daydreams?

- Were you talkative and outgoing or quiet and shy?

Even in childhood, our personalities are continually being influenced by our relationships and the social, physical, and economic environments we live in. At a time when we've not yet built up the defenses necessary to protect our core personalities, we still have to negotiate siblings, school yards, savings accounts, family strife—everything has an impact on how we grow and change.

When you were an adolescent . . .

- Who were the people in your life you admired most? A parent? Teacher? Coach? Friend? What did you admire about them?

- What were your favorite free-time activities?

- Did you fantasize or daydream about your future? What were those dreams?

- Did your parents or others encourage you to pursue any particular career path? Which one? Why did they say it was right for you?

- What were your expectations for what adult life would be like? Where did you imagine you would live? What would you do for a living? What was your fantasy of the good life?
- Were you very social, or more shy?
- What did you like best and least about school?

Adolescence offers most of us the first experience with a vision of the path that our lives should take. Some cultures, like several Native American tribes, have established rituals to encourage these visions. The goal of the Native American vision quest, which involves fasting and spending time alone in the wilderness, allows the individual to discover a vision for himself. In other societies, the opposite is true. In some places, young people's lives are entirely spelled out by their families, including whom they will marry and what they will do for a living. Although freedom of choice was one of the factors that originally drew people from around the world to America, in reality, the degree to which we are encouraged to follow our own visions varies dramatically from person to person, depending a great deal on our families and our cultures.

Do you recall having any vision for yourself as a teen? Did this vision come freely from within you, or was it influenced by others? Did you follow that path, and if so, did it feel like the right one for you? How does it feel now?

As an adult . . .

- Think back over your leisure time and projects at work or school—when did you feel really energized and turned on? What were you doing?
- If you were suddenly told that you had an extra week off, how would you choose to spend that time?

- On a scale of one to one hundred, how much do you prefer to be alone, versus with other people?

- If you didn't have to worry about how much money you'd make, what would you choose to do with your time? What, if any, hobbies are you passionate about?

- When you daydream, what do you daydream about?

- How much do you prefer physical activity to mental tasks?

- Imagine that you had been born a hundred years ago. What do you think your life would have been like? Where do you imagine yourself living? What would you be doing?

- Whom among the people you know do you most admire, and why?

These questions are designed to stimulate your thinking about who you are beneath all the layers of practicality that life places on you. We all face the nitty-gritty issues—what to do for a living, how to pay the bills, where to squeeze in the extra responsibilities we feel obligated to fulfill. The problem comes when these layers of responsibility preoccupy us, blocking a clear assessment of the path we are on and how well that path suits us. Too often we get caught up in *doing*, instead of simply *being*. We lose the sense of whether what we're busy doing actually feels right and makes sense, or if it's just something to distract us from our own unhappiness.

Don't be surprised if you find yourself experiencing some reluctance or discomfort when doing these exercises or contemplating any of these questions. No matter how unhappy we are with the path we are on, we may have mixed feelings about critically examining our life. It can be painful to realize that we've been living someone else's life for a long time. As much as part of us may yearn for a new vision for ourselves, another part of us can fear what having such epiphanies will mean. Visions can be exciting, but they can also upset our apple carts in a big way.

If you find yourself reeling from your vision, don't panic and try not to turn away. The appearance of a vision really means you are now even more in control of your life, not less. Having a vision doesn't mean you have to instantly drop what you've been doing for the past ten, twenty, or thirty years and set off in an entirely new direction. A vision simply shows you a new path, with some new choices you can make. It's like a door opening before you, but it is up to you to decide if you want to pass through or not.

Deciding what, if anything, to do about your vision is as important as having one in the first place. For now, put any reservations you may have on hold and just take some time to reflect. Understand that this exploration can be both exciting and unnerving, but don't let that deter you from pursuing it. Savor the insights you've learned from examining the first question—***Who am I?***—and let them simmer while you turn your attention to the second question: ***Why am I here?***

SECOND QUESTION:

Why Am I Here?

vs.

What Do I Want?

MALCOLM FOUND
HIS PURPOSE

Malcolm's earliest memory was of being snatched from his bed while flames engulfed his home. Four years old, he stood shrieking in his underwear on the sidewalk as the white police and firemen stood idly by, watching his mother dash out of the house with his baby sister in her arms, seconds before the whole house collapsed around them.

Malcolm's family had thought they would escape the threats of the Ku Klux Klan when they moved from Nebraska to Michigan, but the threats only continued, more tangibly and tragically. Two years after the fire, his beloved Baptist minister father was found on the streetcar tracks with his skull crushed. The shock and devastation of her husband's brutal murder was too much for Malcolm's mother to bear—she was committed to a state mental hospital, and her eight children were divided among various foster homes and state institutions.

Although his foster home was peaceful, it couldn't protect Malcolm from the prejudice his father had spoken out against. An excellent student, he'd planned on becoming a lawyer until a high school teacher told him to be "realistic" and plan on becoming a carpenter instead. Shattered and disillusioned, he dropped out of school.

With cunning prowess, he soon developed an extensive gambling operation, a flair for marketing prostitutes, and a serious drug habit. It wasn't long before a newly organized burglary ring landed him in jail.

In prison, the anger at his lot threatened to consume him; fellow inmates even took to calling him Satan because of his infamous temper. But then he discovered the library and soon worked his way through the dictionary, from A to Z, so he could better understand the other books he wanted to read. A change had started to come over him. His temper quieted; he felt pride in gaining control. And then, when a friend told him about Allah, a god who had "360 degrees of knowledge," he knew that he had found his purpose . . . and civil rights leader Malcolm X went on to make history.

Why Am I Here?

In boardrooms all over the world, the sharpest business minds spend hours carefully boiling down the purpose of their company into one distinct message that answers the question *Why are we here?* These vision statements then focus the activities of the company for years, even decades. But how many of us ever do the same thing for our lives?

Motivation is a tricky business. Most often, when we're casting about for something to motivate us, we set goals with rewards, and we focus on what we want and how we're going to get it. We're not alone in this strategy—we're often encouraged by family, friends, bosses, billboards. But think of it—what would the world be like if even one-tenth of us decided that instead of asking *What do I want?* we would ask, **Why am I here?** That instead of viewing our actions through the lens of *desire*, we would select our actions based on our *purpose?*

Let's be honest—the question *What do I want?* will always be with us. We ask it several, even hundreds of times a day—Do I want French toast or pancakes? Do I want a BMW or a Mercedes?

Do I want to watch the news or go to bed? The very economy we've come to rely upon for our prosperity rests on the premise of making people ask themselves this question almost constantly. But that doesn't mean we have to let it determine the direction of our lives. Fulfilling our desires may be fine for the short term, as entertainment or diversion. But when it comes to living a life of real purpose, we must begin from a place we have total control over—our own intentions. When we make these intentions conscious—as when we ask ourselves **Why am I here?**—they become our mission.

LOOKING BEYOND THE LENS OF DESIRE

Now, I'm not here to suggest that we should never ask ourselves what we want. If we didn't, we'd never be able to read a menu or pick out a pair of socks! What I am suggesting is that a life spent in devotion to this question is apt to leave us emotionally empty and chronically hungry, no matter how many things we accumulate.

We all have legitimate needs—shelter, food, and companionship, for example. But in our modern society, we've ventured way beyond these basic desires. The advertising industry, having exhausted all of our basic needs decades ago, has developed into a sophisticated technology for social manipulation—its entire purpose is to create new and artificial needs. With strong appeals to ego, sex, and simple vanity, it leaves very few of us immune to its siren call. Even store layouts are designed to lure customers farther inside, where research has shown they're more likely to make purchases.

Viewed through this lens of desire, life appears before us as a tantalizing and ever-changing smorgasbord of new and better things, offered as replacements for the old and presumably inferior things we already have. When we only ask ourselves *What do I want?* we're led to a life of insatiable craving, envy, and chronic dissatisfaction. No sooner do we have what we think we want, we ask ourselves, yet again, *What do I want **now**?*

Going through our lives constantly seeking to answer the question *What do I want?* is very similar to going through life trying to answer the question *Who should I be?* Both questions push our focus *outward.* Just as *Who should I be?* invites us to depend on others for our identity, *What do I want?* leads us to define ourselves in terms of our desires, which are also easily influenced by outside forces.

Friedrich Nietzsche asked, "Is not life a hundred times too short for us to bore ourselves?" And what is boredom if not the lack of purpose? Let's face it, doesn't the endless consumer treadmill get a little old after a while?

When we ask **Why am I here?** we immediately experience a radical shift in the way we see ourselves in relation to the world. Life no longer appears as an overwhelming smorgasbord whose various dishes compete for our attention and trigger our cravings. When we ask this question, life loses some of its material aspect, taking on, instead, a more spiritual one. Our attention moves away from possessions and turns toward close relationships, deep engagement with nature, or perhaps even a newly formed concept of a higher power. **Why am I here?** challenges us to view ourselves in the context of humankind, to look within, to seek a deeper way of defining ourselves. We find ourselves moving from *craving* to *meaning* as a basis for living, and with that shift, we find an enormous wellspring of energy and motivation. Once we derive our motivation from something that continually refuels our connection to others and our soul, it's like a circle that just keeps replenishing itself. We've tapped into an infinite life force that breeds happiness in a way no possession ever could. Max experienced just this type of shift.

MAX'S STORY: FROM DESIRE TO DEEPER MEANING

Imagine valuing your life so little that you're willing to throw it away on a horse race. That's the point where Max was before he experienced his quantum change.

Max worked for fifteen years as an engineer for a major oil company, rising fairly quickly through the ranks to a position in the company's international division. Along the way, he accumulated two of everything he ever thought he wanted—including two mistresses. But he still wasn't happy or excited about life. He regularly risked his marriage—and his life—with gambling, drinking, and fooling around. If it was reckless, Max did it. He probably would've continued on this path until he was penniless, or dead, or both, but shortly after he returned to the States from a six-month stint abroad, Max got a call that would change his life.

Max hadn't seen his younger brother, Brian, in well over a year. Growing up, Max had always seemed to easily tower over his brother. Max was naturally brilliant in school; Brian had learning disabilities and labored over his studies. Max was athletic; Brian seemed clumsy in comparison. Max got into a prestigious technical college, graduated with an engineering degree, and immediately got onto the corporate fast track; Brian got an associate's degree from a community college and worked as a licensed practical nurse in a local hospital and at a nursing home. Both brothers married, but while Max remained childless and without any desire for kids, Brian married his high-school sweetheart and promptly had two sons.

After moving away from home, Max saw less and less of his family, small as it was. His parents were still alive and active, comfortably settled into a senior community about an hour's drive from Brian and his family. On most holidays, Max's parents and Brian's family got together, but Max and his wife would show up only occasionally at these gatherings. Max usually forgot birthdays and anniversaries, but when he did remember, and he happened to be coming by, he brought extravagant gifts.

Wake-Up Call

The call came just after three o'clock in the morning. Max's wife picked up the phone and roused Max from a heavy, post-drinking sleep. Through his foggy haze, Max heard his father's voice on the line. His words seemed heavy and strained. "Your brother was in an accident tonight, Max. He's critical," he said. "I think you'd better get up here as soon as you can."

Max threw on clothes with a stone in his stomach. Pushing his expensive car to the limit, he and his wife made the normally four-hour drive in a little over three. The sun was rising as he pulled into the hospital parking lot.

When they got to Brian's room in the intensive care unit, Max rushed up to the side of his brother's bed, unable to speak. Brian's eyes were closed, his head was heavily bandaged, and his body was connected to what seemed like a hundred tubes and monitors. Time stopped. The family surrounded the bed while a nurse adjusted an intravenous drip and a doctor studied Brian's chart, his expression grave. Their father turned to Max and whispered, "He had a brain hemorrhage."

No more than a minute later, Brian's eyes opened suddenly and his body stiffened, startling everyone. Max thought Brian looked up at him as he drew in a deep breath. Brian died then, quietly and seemingly without pain. The next second, the air was pierced with high-pitched beeps and whistles that made everyone jump. The family was whisked aside as a crash cart was rushed up to Brian's bedside. To no avail.

To Max, Brian's death seemed to have happened on another planet. "It was more like a dream than a real memory," Max said. "Even now, when I dream about the Brian I knew when we were growing up, those dreams seem more real than the reality of his death."

Max had had drinking and gambling problems well before his brother's death, but they got much worse afterward. These habits had always been a sore point between Max and his wife. They argued more and more often, but even as he saw her drifting away from him, he could not summon the energy to change his ways. One day she found out that he'd bet—and lost—four thousand dollars on a horse race. That was the last straw for her. Six months after Brian's death, Max's wife filed for divorce and quickly settled for the house—which had some equity—in lieu of alimony, fearing that Max would end up bankrupt and unable to pay. She wasn't far off. Even though Max managed to hold on to his lucrative job, the money went out faster than it came in.

The Road to Quantum Change

The Christmas after his brother's death, following his divorce, Max went to visit his parents. Brian's wife, Jennifer, was there, along with Brian's two sons. It was a sad holiday gathering, but it triggered a vision that would change Max's life.

"At the end of the day, as I was driving home, I suddenly realized that I had no desire to go home at all," said Max. "All I wanted to do was turn around and drive back to my parents' place." He kept driving home, but in that strong impulse hid the burgeoning seed of Max's vision.

"The next morning, when I drove my brand-new car to work, I suddenly saw it for what it was—an obvious status symbol that drew a lot of eyes my way," he said. "I realized that I took no pleasure in owning or driving it, no matter how expensive it was. Then I opened the door to my office and walked in, sat down behind my big, expensive desk, looked around, and realized that I felt empty. Completely, totally empty."

That empty feeling clung to Max for days. Then, a week later, he did something he hadn't done in decades: He called his parents and asked if he could visit. He was taking some time off and he wanted to know if would it be okay if he sacked out on the fold-out couch in their family room for a couple of nights. "Of course," his mother said.

The couple of nights extended to a week, and in that time Max didn't drink at all. He saw his two nephews twice that week, and before he left he invited them to spend a weekend at his place. Each day, he was beginning to develop more of a sense of where he was heading.

"On the drive home, I remember feeling genuinely happy for the first time in a long, long time," he said. "I was looking forward to my nephews' visiting me. I realized that for my entire adult life up to that point, I'd been devoted to pursuing things. At the age of forty I had already acquired and lost more material things than most people collect in a lifetime, but I was well on my way to dying of alcoholism. I had so little respect for myself, I'd been willing to sacrifice my marriage to a horse race."

While he was mulling over his past, his mind offered up a picture: He actually envisioned himself betting his wife for the horse. That one image drove everything home for him—in that moment, Max saw his life clearly for the first time. What Max had discovered was that viewing life through the lens of desire and constantly seeking the answer to the question *What do I want?* ultimately breeds an empty life. In the aftermath of his brother's death, Max had begun to ask himself **Why am I here?** His primary motivation was shifting from satisfying his desires to finding meaning and purpose.

One sign that he'd had a true visionary experience—one that could trigger a quantum change in his lifestyle—was that the plans it inspired had depth and resilience. Over the next two years, Max literally remade his life. The changes he made fit together into a profoundly different, coherent whole. Some changes took time, planning, and persistence, but they were all linked to the same primary concept that helped him find a purpose for his life.

A New Direction

The first thing Max did was initiate the process of changing careers. Having experienced the destructive power of addictions, he decided to pursue a career helping people overcome them or prevent them from ever taking hold. By that time, Max hadn't had a drink or placed a bet in over a year. Instead of spending his money impulsively and frivolously, he discovered that he actually preferred living frugally. He discovered that he had a latent talent for cooking and he enjoyed preparing his own meals way more than eating out five or six times a week.

To help finance his education, Max sold most of his more-extravagant possessions. The first things to go were the flashy car and two sets of custom golf clubs that he'd bought on impulse and now found embarrassingly ostentatious. In a year, Max was able to save enough money to quit his job and go to school full time. He threw himself into his studies with gusto, but whenever a break came along, no matter how brief, he returned home to spend time with his family.

During one of his visits to his nephews, Max had another powerful experience. One of the boys asked him to help him repair a chair whose rear legs had come loose; Max said he'd love to, but didn't have much experience or any tools. "No problem," said his nephew. "Come downstairs!"

There in the basement, largely undisturbed for two years, was a complete woodworking shop full of hand and power tools, still as neat as Brian had left it—save for a substantial accumulation of dust. "It just took my breath away," said Max. "I suddenly remembered that when Brian and I were kids we'd tried to build things. We built a tree house once, even tried to make chairs." Max laughed and shook his head at the memory. "Some chairs! We sat in them and they collapsed at almost the same time!"

Max had long since abandoned any interest he had in building things, but Brian had apparently pursued his. Max helped to fix his nephews' ailing chair, then spent another hour alone in the basement, looking around his brother's shop, dusting off the equipment, picking up tools and examining them. He offered Jennifer extravagant prices for the tools, which she steadfastly refused. But she said that Max was welcome to borrow any or all of them for as long as he wished. After that day, Max decided to limit his job search to within an hour of his nephews and the rest of his family.

Max's reintroduction to woodworking also revived a long-neglected passion. Although he couldn't paint or draw well himself, he had many friends who were artists, and he'd always been struck by how much a good frame could add to a painting. He started making frames for friends, who in turn referred other friends, and a mini cottage industry was born. One of Max's nephews expressed an interest in helping him, and the two started working together, nicely combining two of the most important facets of his vision: connection and creativity.

THE STAGES OF QUANTUM CHANGE

Many people experience their visions in gradually unfolding stages, like Max did. His process of quantum change began with a vision that was spurred by his brother's death. Tragic as it was, that dark night had opened a door for Max, inviting him to take a fresh look at himself and his life. The next phase in his vision came after his Christmas visit, when Max realized that he felt empty and had a strong impulse to turn around and head back to his parents' home. The third part of the vision came when Max descended into his brother's basement and rediscovered both a link to his past and a key to his future.

But Max didn't just sit around, pondering and contemplating—he got out there and did the work, tried out his visions to see if they would fly. Rarely does simply asking ourselves the question *Why am I here?* lead us to either a conclusive or a quick answer—we have to be willing to do a little digging, too. Passively waiting for enlightenment can be very frustrating. To help the process along, try the following exercises to stimulate and guide your thinking toward finding an answer to this important question.

Chronicle Your Desires

One exercise you may find helpful involves making a list of the different things you've wanted at different times in your life, starting with childhood and working your way forward. Draw the chart below in your journal to use as a guide for creating your own chronicle of desire.

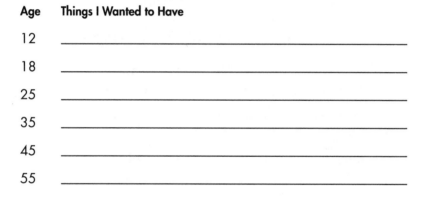

Chronicle of Desire

Age	Things I Wanted to Have
12	
18	
25	
35	
45	
55	

To begin, find a quiet spot in your house and close the door. Give yourself about twenty minutes to complete the exercise—more, if you have it. (Note: If you find yourself getting stuck, don't attempt to complete this exercise in a single sitting—spread it out over several days to give your unconscious time to find new memories.)

First, close your eyes and create a mental image of what you were like as a child. What did you look like when you were **eleven or twelve** years old? Picture the friends you hung out with and what you did together. Reconstruct the neighborhood you lived in, the school you went to, the smell of the bus, or the sound of the playground, and place yourself inside those moments. Jot down the most resonant images in your journal. Now try to recall some of the things you wanted most when you were a kid—a toy, a bike, a friend? Transfer this list onto the chart.

Now, fast-forward your memory to when you were about **eighteen** years old. What was your life like then? For most people, that would correspond to their senior year in high school, although others may have been in college or working by that time. What were you doing at eighteen? What did you look like, and what kinds of clothes did you like to wear? What were your personal goals at that point in your life, and what (aside from sex!) did you desire most—a car, a guitar, freedom?

By age **twenty-five**, many of us have already set a general course in life. What was your emerging lifestyle when you were in your mid-twenties? How were you spending the bulk of your time? Did you feel that you were working toward some goal, or did your life seem stuck or stalled, even at that tender age? What, if any, opportunities presented themselves to you at the time, and did you seize any of them? Finally, what things—a house, a challenging career, a raise, a spouse—did you desire most when you were a young adult?

Imagine now that you are **thirty-something**. Can you picture yourself? Where are you living, and what are you doing? Are you working, going to school, raising a family? Are you basically happy with the direction of your life? If not, what seems to be missing? What are the things you desire most?

As you work your way forward through the years, from childhood to the present, use your imagination to picture yourself, your environment, the life you were living, and the things you remember wanting most. Then, when you are finished recording your desires, answer the following questions underneath your chronicle of desire.

- Is there any discernible pattern in your lists of the things you wanted? Do they get longer as time goes on? Do the material items on your list become more and more expensive over time?

- What influenced the things you've wanted? Were they things your friends had? Were they things you saw advertised?

- What percentage of your lists consists of *material* things, as opposed to nonmaterial things, such as wanting a girlfriend or boyfriend, a spouse, a more satisfying job, or children?

- At any stage in your life, did you believe that having material things would somehow make you happy?

- How much, in your estimation, have your desires for *things* controlled your life? How much time and effort have gone into pursuing *things* that you thought would make you happy?

Again, keep this information in mind as you think about the question **Why am I here?** Are you starting to see these desires in a new light? Circle any insights you find particularly important, and keep them in mind for when you devise your own answers to the six questions.

Write Your Own Eulogy

Admittedly, at first thought, writing your own eulogy sounds a bit morbid. But when we approach it in the spirit of a historian, it can be very enlightening and fun. Instead of focusing on your death, imagine that you've been asked to celebrate the entire life of someone you love and admire—only this someone is you. Picture the people in the audience at your memorial service, family and loved ones as well as total strangers. In this scenario, given a hundred percent latitude, what would you have done in your life? How would you have lived? What would you like to hear said about you? What would you most like to be remembered for?

The course of history is marked by many individuals whose motivation shifted at some point, away from the pursuit of wealth and material gain and toward a concern with meaning and purpose. Philanthropists from John Rockefeller and Andrew Carnegie to Bill Gates and Ted Turner act as if they had done this very exercise. They've clearly concluded that they'd not only like to be remembered for how much money they had or how much land they owned, but how much they helped. Mother Teresa was moved throughout her life to answer the question *Why am I here?* Mahatma Gandhi struggled unhappily as a lawyer until he asked himself the question *Why am I here?*—this shift changed not only his life but also the destinies of millions of his countrypeople.

Few of us are in the financial position of a Rockefeller or a Gates, and altruism and moral courage on the level of Mother Teresa's and Gandhi's are rare indeed. Still, for all of us, the basic question remains: What mark will I leave behind?

Assess Your Relationships

When we ask ourselves *What do I want?* we usually think of material things, but not always. Some people remember that what they wanted most as a child was not some toy, or a bigger room, but for their divorced parents to reconcile, an unemployed parent to find a job, or a sick parent to get well. Others have told me that, as teenagers, what they wanted most was a boyfriend or girlfriend—or just a friend, period.

Looking at our relationships turns out to be another helpful way to try on a different set of psychological lenses and look at our lives in terms of why we are here, instead of what we want. Take a moment to answer the following questions in your notebook.

- Which relationships are most important to you now, and why?

- How would your own life be different if you were to lose one or another of these relationships?

- What contribution do you make to these relationships? In other words, how would these people's lives be different if they did not have their relationship with you?

You'll address your relationships more thoroughly in the fourth and fifth questions, but I bring this up here to help underscore the differences between longing for material goods and longing for connection. While material desires are always about possession, relationships are a constant negotiation, a give and take that defies all sense of proprietary claim. Because we cannot *own* other people, we keep them close to us by *loving* them, as legitimate a mission and purpose as I can imagine. John Lennon encouraged us to "Imagine no possessions." If that came true, what would our desires mean? What would be left to do but simply love one another?

Identify with Your Heroes

Ask around—I doubt you will find one person who talks about having a hero whom he admires simply because that hero became rich. Sure, we may admire people who made successes out of their lives, but when asked why we admire these people, we rarely talk about money. Instead, we talk about people's triumphs over adversity, their spirit, their genius, their perseverance and determination, their generosity or philanthropy.

Think back on all the people who have been heroes to you throughout your life. As you list each one, write the approximate age at which you identified that person as your hero. Leave a few spaces between each to answer the following questions.

- What three qualities do you admire in each of these people?
- In what ways have you modeled yourself after your hero? In what ways can you see yourself in him or her?
- What experiences have they had that were similar to your own?
- If you had to ask each hero for one bit of advice about your life, what might it be?

Get Involved

The comedian Bill Cosby used to joke about the experiences of his fellow college students when they smoked marijuana. Under the influence of this drug, he said, many of his friends suddenly discovered the meaning of life, along with a way to touch their elbows with the hand on the same arm. Of course, by the next morning both insights had mysteriously evaporated.

Mr. Cosby's own life has been a testament to the pursuit of meaning and purpose, from his decision to seek a doctorate in education to his charitable work. For me, the lesson in both Cosby's joke and in his own life is this: The answer to *Why am I here?* is best sought by being engaged in life. You're not likely to discover it through altered states of consciousness or by withdrawing from the world.

Here are some simple suggestions for staying engaged with the world instead of retreating from it. Write down each heading in your journal and brainstorm two ways you'd like to try each. For now, don't think about time restrictions or lack of resources—this is a resource list you can draw from later.

Volunteer: People often say they themselves benefit more from volunteering than the people they help do. There is a tremendous need in our society for people to volunteer their services in any number of areas: teaching literacy, mentoring youths, coaching young athletes, staffing food kitchens. Being involved opens you up to new perspectives and imbues the simple acts of cooking, reading, or playing games with a world of purpose and meaning.

Experiment: Write a list of new activities that you've always wanted to try but never had the time, money, or courage to do: join a cultural organization, learn to juggle or paint, travel somewhere you've never been. Broadening the scope of your experiences will expose new sides of yourself that you may not know exist.

Read: Reading biographies of people who have made an impact on the world can be another way to learn about your heroes, find new ones, and expose yourself to the stories of people whose lives have been driven by vision. Who are some people you want to learn more about?

Now, read over the list in your journal. Circle two activities that really speak to you. Make a commitment to yourself to try one of them *this week* and the second one *this month*. Revisit this list at the beginning of each month to select again, to keep reminding yourself to ask *Why am I here?*—a question that can grow and expand with each asking.

Stepping Off the Treadmill

Discovering an answer to the question *Why am I here?* can be incredibly invigorating. The answer will inevitably add balance to what may have been the exclusive pursuit of money, status, or material possessions. While none of us ever intends to become materialistic, it can be an incredible act of defiance to step off the consumer treadmill for even one moment to catch our breath. Asking the question *Why am I here?* gives us permission to find satisfaction through our relationships and our life's truest mission instead of next year's model.

Like Max, you may discover that when you change your lenses, your priorities shift, automatically and dramatically. A life that has been stalled may suddenly be reenergized; if you've been going in circles, wondering how to move ahead, you may suddenly see, with total clarity, the right direction to go in. Whether it occurs in a flash, as it happened for Sally, or more gradually, as was the case for Max, the revealing of your vision will almost certainly involve a profound shift in your goals and your priorities.

Most of us are simply too busy, caught up in just living day to day, to take time to consciously ask ourselves why we're living the way we are. Often we're seeking the answers to the wrong questions about the *way* we are living. There is a critical difference between a life spent pursuing desires and a life that is lived in pursuit of purpose and meaning.

Once we've asked ourselves the question, it's time to put that life into the broader context of community. The third question—*Where do I belong?*—will do just that.

THIRD QUESTION:

Where Do I Belong?

vs.

What Is My Position?

PAUL CAME HOME
TO HIMSELF

Paul was born into a liberal Parisian family during the mid-nineteenth century. Despite the family's middle-class lifestyle, his parents thought anything was better than living under the rule of Louis Napoleon. So they set off for Peru, the land of his mother's people. The family spent four years in South America, and when they returned to Orleans, France, Paul was miserable. The town's oppressive conformity and suburban lifestyle clashed with his burgeoning passion for the vibrant colors of the tropics and the thrill of travel.

His thirst for adventure would remain unquenched until he was seventeen and could join the merchant marine. After six years at sea with the marines and the navy, his wanderlust seemingly sated, Paul got a job with a leading Paris stockbroker and settled into a comfortable, middle-class existence like that of his parents. He married a Danish woman and they moved from a nice apartment in the city to a spacious house in the outskirts of Paris where they raised five children together. By the time he was thirty-five, Paul had money, a solid business reputation, and a family who loved him.

On the weekends, he dabbled in his painting hobby, visiting art shows and even buying some work from professional artists. Although he took several lessons, mostly he learned by studying others and practicing his own style.

When the stock market crashed and his trading career took a turn for the worse, Paul realized that his "secure" existence was no sure bet. That realization spurred him to pitch his stable career to devote himself entirely to his painting. He eventually sold thirty paintings to fund his voyage to Tahiti and the South Seas, where he lived and painted for the rest of his life . . . and that man was Postimpressionist painter Paul Gauguin.

Where Do I Belong?

If Americans could choose only one credo, it would probably be *Don't Fence Me In.* As a culture, we tend to resist rootedness because we find it too limiting. We celebrate the renegade and the cowboy. *Don't try to tell me where I belong,* we say. *I'll find my home, home on the range. I'm going west, young man.*

To a certain extent, this wanderlust and rejection of roots built our country, and our resistance to tradition continues to fuel the entrepreneurial spirit that drives the economy. Many of us think nothing of picking up stakes and moving across state lines to garner that extra ten thousand, that IPO promise, that shot at the vice presidency. But what if the position we're drawn to is not in the place where we feel at home?

Developing a solid sense of our place in the world is an integral part of defining who we are. In modern society, the most common way we ask ourselves this question is, *What is my position?* When I ask people this question, they usually have no problem answering—they immediately respond by telling me their job title or their profession. They conveniently define their place as their role in some corporate or social hierarchy, saying, "I'm a factory worker," "I'm a stockbroker," or "I'm a stay-at-home mom."

There are two big problems with the question *What is my position?* First, it causes us to identify solely with our work; second, it places us in a pecking order, as some positions traditionally have higher status than others—status that can also be ripped away at a moment's notice. Contrast this with the third question, **Where do I belong?** When we ask ourselves this question, we are immediately rooted in something real and lasting: our connection to loved ones, to our traditions, and to the place we feel most ourselves. **Where do I belong?** can make us think of a specific town or city, the call of a mountain or an ocean, or even the loving connection of a certain circle of friends or a community center. **Where do I belong?** doesn't seek to "put us in our place"—instead, it opens its arms to welcome us back home.

THE MOBILE SOCIETY

Over the past three generations, the driving force of the economy has moved quickly from stable, rooted manufacturing plants and corporations toward transient information-based products and services. The former institutions used to form the core of many towns, affording people a measure of steadiness in their lives. When it came to their sense of place, men and women could identify with their communities, their churches or spiritual centers, their neighbors and friends, their families, even the land they lived on—*plus* the companies they worked for and the positions they held there.

As recently as the 1960s, it was not unusual for an employee to spend his or her entire career with one company. Longevity was celebrated, and pins commemorating ten, twenty, and thirty years

of service were worn with pride on lapels or shirt pockets. Retirement was a big deal, and retirement dinners would invariably be
attended by senior executives. But who among us today can honestly say that they feel any mutual commitment between themselves and their employers? How many employers today truly
honor longevity? What corporation today would hesitate to let go
of senior employees in order to meet profit targets? And this lack
of loyalty is a two-way street—most employees don't hesitate to
jump ship as soon as a better offer comes along.

This instability and change are now the rule rather than the
exception. Whereas it was once considered acceptable to live in the
same community your entire life, today we're tempted to see this
as unhealthy, stagnant, limiting. We view resistance to change as a
personal problem, an impediment to corporate growth, and the
death knell for personal advancement. We are all expected to accept and even embrace continual change. But what happens when
this slavish devotion to change no longer suits us—what do we do
then?

The Limitations of Rank

One good reason not to identify our sense of place too much
with our position, then, is that lack of permanence. At some point,
the companies we work for will probably expect us to pick up our
families and move, or else leave. Most likely we will begin to worry
about our job security when profits fall, or when our seniority
makes us a high-priced item in the corporate budget.

This insecurity only heightens our tendency to place ourselves
in a hierarchy and compare ourselves to others around us. Focusing on position always injects an element of competition and
status into the process of defining our place—we are either richer

or poorer, white collar or blue collar, supervisor or underling, housewife or working mother, and so on. Our positions depend on other people being either "above" or "below" us. We look outside ourselves, instead of within ourselves, for definition and validation of who we are.

An alternative lens on our sense of place would be one that invites us to *identify* with others rather than compare ourselves to them. **Where do I belong?** gives us this perspective, immediately coaxing us to draw associations and links to others. Although the world may press us to define ourselves by rank and status, when it comes to quantum change, locating ourselves among like minds is way more likely to elicit a vision than distancing ourselves from others in competition. When we think about where we belong, we learn to embrace who we are, rather than reject our natural impulses for connection. We grow and expand our ability to love and appreciate our bonds. Ultimately, we get so much more enjoyment and satisfaction out of our lives. Read on for the stories of Pam and Ken, two people for whom **Where do I belong?** became the critical question in learning to balance their drive to achieve with their yearning to belong.

PAM'S STORY: STEPPING OFF THE RELOCATION MERRY-GO-ROUND

The longest way 'round is the shortest way home. Although Pam didn't know it yet, this proverb held the key to her vision. Thirty-four years old, attractive, and successful, Pam should have been enjoying the prime of her life, but instead she found herself stuck, professionally and personally.

What impressed me most when I first met Pam was her intensity. She was short and slender, yet she came across as quite powerful. Talking to her, you could feel the energy simmering beneath the surface, but her eyes were sad and her face was lined with tension. "Frankly, my life seems to have stalled," she said. "I feel like I'm at sea."

By far the biggest focus of Pam's life was her job. Pam had carved out a career based on hard work, a talent for motivating others, and plenty of determination. She credited her drive to her working-class family, where a strong work ethic was a virtue. "If something had to be done, we just did it. Nobody got a free ride," she said.

Starting out with only a high-school education, she'd worked her way up from an entry-level position as a department store salesperson to senior management for the chain. Along the way, she'd completed a bachelor's degree in business administration, graduating with honors. During those fifteen years, this busy woman had also moved seven times. Although she was now working in the organization's headquarters and had been there for nearly a year, Pam's bosses still expected her to travel fairly often, and even to relocate for periods of up to six months at a time. When the company opened a new store, or when an existing store was having financial problems, Pam was one of a select few who could take a lead role.

Pam's high-energy, pitch-in-and-do-it personality was a good fit for her firm's corporate culture. She saw herself not just as a manager who trained and monitored performance, but as a coach, building and motivating teams to do their best. Careful not to mix business with pleasure, she didn't socialize outside of work with any of the people she supervised because she felt that that could make correcting or disciplining them more awkward than it already was. Combined with her frequent moves and long hours, this policy turned Pam into something of a loner. She had a small handful of friends, only one of whom she regularly saw face to face. Although she earned an excellent salary, she had not accumulated many possessions, primarily because it was so inconvenient to move them. Things invariably got broken, so she'd resigned herself to traveling light and practicing a "less to lose" lifestyle.

One of the reasons for Pam's unhappiness, ironically enough, was her success. Work dominated her life and had for some time. But her niche at the top of the corporate hierarchy left her feeling isolated and alone. She put up barriers or even pulled away from men she dated, trying to stave off the inevitable pain that resulted when they drifted apart after her relocations. Pam was a classic case of someone who could easily answer the question *What is my position?* but had no idea how to answer **Where do I belong?**

Look Homeward, Angel

Pam admitted that she'd never really thought about her own sense of place, but she promised to take some time to mull the question over. After a few weeks of playing with the idea, she came back to my office, very excited.

"When I thought about where I belong, my mind kept wandering back to my younger years. I even dreamed about my childhood for the first time in ages," she said. "I realized that from the time I was a young child through high-school graduation, I felt like I actually belonged where I was."

Pam spent those years in the suburbs of Providence, Rhode Island, the only daughter in a close-knit Italian family. "I was my father's little princess. He was very protective of me and spoiled me

as much as he could afford to," she said, smiling. "On the other
hand, my family—my father, especially—had different rules for my
two brothers than for me. Basically that meant that they got away
with a whole lot more than I did."

The one thing Pam had always wished were different was her
family's expectations for the way she'd live her life. "When I was
in high school, a couple of my female cousins were talking about
going to college, about becoming teachers. When I brought it up
with my parents, they made it clear that they expected me to
marry an Italian boy from Providence—preferably a successful
one—and to spend the rest of my life raising children and keeping
house.

"I know they're disappointed that I didn't fulfill their dream.
They always introduce me as their 'educated' daughter, or 'our
daughter the executive.' They smile, but there's a definite edge.
They'd much rather introduce me as 'Mrs. So-and-So' and show
off two or three grandchildren." Those expectations had driven
Pam away almost immediately after she graduated from high
school. She had taken the job at the department store and had
never looked back.

That departure from home let her see a lot of the world, but
the physical distance also allowed a more critical separation to take
place: By moving out of Providence, Pam had broken out of the
box her parents sought to place her in and said goodbye to her
younger, more dependent self. Now an accomplished executive,
Pam had claimed her fortune, but she wanted to bring back that
lost sense of community that had surrounded her as a child.
Thanks to the third question—***Where do I belong?***—Pam was beginning to realize that she *could* go home again and recapture her

treasured roots. She would just be coming home a stronger, more independent person than the one who left.

Pam's Road to Quantum Change

That clear memory of her childhood sense of belonging marked the dawn of Pam's vision and started her on the road to quantum change, but it didn't cancel out her earlier decisions to pursue her education and career. They were built on that strong foundation. Pam's long path had brought her first to her truest self, the self she could then bring home to share with her family. She could now rediscover her sense of place without having to sacrifice the career and the independence she'd worked so hard to build.

After giving it careful thought, Pam decided to return to Providence—not to the suburbs where she was raised, but to the city itself, which had recently undergone a renaissance and was now one of the most desirable places to live on the East Coast. Although her dad had died a few years earlier, her mom, brothers, and cousins and their families were still living in the surrounding areas. In Pam's new vision, she lived close enough for family to stop by once a week, but not once a day.

She met with her supervisors and leveled with them: The nomadic life wasn't working for her anymore, but she had a plan. She would return to Providence and make it her home base, continuing to travel as necessary. However, she did not want to relocate entirely, even if the assignment took six months or longer. Instead, she'd willingly accept any assignments given to her if all efforts would be made to focus her assignments in the New England area so she could commute home on weekends. If an assignment took her out of state, she proposed working a four-day week, then flying home on weekends, an arrangement that would still cost the company less than renting her a suite for three to six months at a time.

Pam's superiors listened patiently and after a brief meeting, quickly agreed to her proposal—they definitely didn't want to lose such a star leader. She was ecstatic, as was her family. Instead of hitting her suddenly, Pam's vision had unfolded slowly, but it still shared all the characteristics of a true vision: It reflected a shift in priorities and a consequent change in her life's course; its pieces fit together to form a coherent whole; and it energized her, lifted her from depression, and gave her a sense of peace that had been missing from her life for a long time. She had her career, her hard-won independence, *and* a place where she knew she belonged. She was home, and she was happy.

KEN'S STORY: NEW JOB, UNEXPECTED PROBLEMS

High-performing people who are driven to excel are often, by necessity, very focused. But the same focus that can help them scale the corporate ladder can also lead to a tunnel vision that blocks out everything else. Much like Pam, Ken had been keeping his eye on the prize of a top-level career for more than a decade. He'd changed jobs four times in just over ten years, and each time, he'd been recruited away by a competing firm offering a substantial increase in salary. But when he started his newest position—a coup by any industry standard—he began to feel depressed and confused, and he couldn't figure out why.

Up until now, Ken had been a success all his life. He'd married Mary Beth, his college sweetheart, and the two had a beautiful boy and girl. Finishing at the top of his graduate-school class in both engineering and business administration, Ken had been on the corporate fast track ever since. From the outside, he had a life many would envy—but clearly something was amiss inside.

Soon after he'd started his new job, Ken was assigned as team leader of a diverse group of highly skilled professionals who were charged with developing a cutting-edge high-tech product—just the kind of challenge Ken loved. Excited by the great opportunity, he told Mary Beth he couldn't wait to jump in with both feet—but he soon learned that his new company expected him to jump in up to his *hips*.

The first time he met with the members of his team—none of whom were newcomers to the company—Ken felt like he'd stumbled into an alternative universe. While he was no stranger to long hours, these people took it to a new level. "They eat, sleep, and breathe work!" he said. The whole team was connected by computers, both at home and at work, as is de rigeur in the computer industry. But instead of using this connectivity to be more efficient, his team seemed to fuse into a clingy, dysfunctional virtual family. Team members would compulsively update each other on their work progress, rambling on incessantly, even chatting about opinions on restaurants, minivans, family therapists. Some messages were dated after 10 P.M. on Saturday nights. Ken limited himself to checking his e-mail twice a weekend, but each time, the torrents of responses would overwhelm him. He grew increasingly irritated—these people were spending as much time reading their e-mail as they spent interacting with their families! He was used to working hard, but he resented the crumbling boundaries between his personal and professional lives.

In this case, though, his resistance was futile. When several members of the team confronted him one Monday morning, wondering why he hadn't responded to their weekend missives, Ken reluctantly relinquished his treasured weekends and evenings to check his e-mail. Soon, he found himself spending up to several hours a day reading and responding.

Trying to retain some semblance of sanity, Ken had decided he would respond to his e-mail the way he always had: If someone asked for his opinion, he'd give it; if they asked a technical question, he'd respond. But he wouldn't elaborate, much less spend time chatting about other issues. He thought he was saving time—he didn't realize he was losing his team's faith.

Disappointment and Surprise

A little less than four months into the project, Ken was called in to speak with his boss. As he walked into the office, he was taken aback to see two senior executives also waiting for him. After some initial pleasantries, they got right down to business—they told him that his team was not performing up to the company's expectations. Ken's palms started to sweat as they detailed their complaints: They'd expected such an experienced team to have "gelled" much better and to have produced results already. They worried that the company might be losing its edge to the competition in developing the new product.

Stunned and mentally scrambling for an explanation, Ken was about to respond by bringing up his team's unusual work habits when his superiors revealed the negative results of a routine corporate poll of the members of his team, usually performed a month into every project. Some of his team members described Ken as cool and remote. For the first time in Ken's life, his job performance was not up to expectations, but the reason completely baffled him—were they saying that he was supposed to get *personally* close to the men and women who reported to him? He tried to contain his surprise, but he was shaken. Seeing his discomfort, the supervisors tried to end the meeting on an upbeat note, but what they had to say was of little solace. "You've got a wealth of technical skill, and that's why we brought you on board, Ken," one executive said. "We think you just need to learn more about our work ethic. It's obvious that you're not used to how we do things. We want you to succeed here—when you succeed, we all succeed."

Ken felt humiliated and shaken, betrayed by his team, and, most of all, trapped. This company was one of the most successful in its field and had a history of turning out superior products in record time, along with the profits to prove it. Bailing out now, or losing the race to the competition, could seriously damage his career. He had to make it work.

A Family Problem

To make matters worse, things were also in full meltdown mode at home. At first Mary Beth had shared Ken's enthusiasm about his new job, even though it meant another move. The increase in Ken's salary would allow them not only to save for the kids' college, but also to start investing. They'd always made joint decisions about Ken's career and moving the family, and together they'd made it work.

But this time, Mary Beth, who'd taken on their many moves with unending energy and resilience, had slipped into a depression. She'd had down periods in the past, but she would always get better over time, not worse. Ken was concerned for her, but he really needed her support. He couldn't help feeling a little let down. Both his teams seemed to be unraveling around him.

For her part, Mary Beth was doing her best to keep it together—she was now going to weekly therapy sessions and taking antidepressant and sleeping pills. Ken's upbeat, fun-loving partner had been transformed into someone who could do little more than watch TV and go to bed early. Though the relationship remained strong, the two laughed a lot less, held each other less often, and practically stopped having sex.

Mary Beth was not the only one spiraling downward. Their older child, Adam, had always been an academic star and a popular kid among his peers, but now his grades were slipping and he seemed to be having trouble making friends. Ken sensed a growing distance between them—they'd had a close relationship, but lately his son was cold and removed and spent a lot of time in his room. At this point, the only bright spot in Ken's life was Morgan, his six-year-old daughter. Cheery, energetic, and affectionate, Morgan remained her dad's biggest fan—but in his darker moments, he wondered when that would change, too.

How had this happened? Why was Ken's life suddenly coming apart at the seams? The challenges he was facing, at work and in his personal life, were more related to one another than he thought. Sadly, what he didn't know was not only hurting him, but those he loved as well. The torment clouding his life had nothing to do with Ken's intelligence, motivation, values, or commitment. In his fervor to chase the American dream, Ken had somehow gotten lost and was floating adrift—and he was taking his family with him.

Understanding the Issue

Ken could easily tell me what his position was, and his entire identity and the destiny of his family were based on it. In contrast, he got noticeably uncomfortable when I asked him where he belonged. He didn't want to be pigeonholed, and he couldn't under-

stand what the question had to do with his situation. But later that evening, Ken shared the question *Where do I belong?* with Mary Beth, and her reaction surprised him.

"You know, Ken, I think that may be a big part of my problem, and maybe Adam's problem, too," she told him. "Between moving around the country so many times and your being pressured to work all the time, I'm not sure I know where I belong. I wouldn't be surprised if Adam felt the same way."

When they brought Adam into the living room to talk about it, he admitted that it was hard to be in his fourth school. He didn't want to make new friends again, and working hard in school wasn't fun anymore. He really missed the last place they lived. "I even dream about it sometimes," he confessed to his tearful parents.

Adam's dream was the spark Ken needed to understand the crux of his problem. Just like his son, Ken was also reluctant to fit in with the new kids, primarily because the corporate culture he was being asked to embrace just didn't feel like a place where he belonged. "We've become a family without roots," said Ken. "We've lived in very nice communities, but we haven't belonged in any of them. My career has turned us into vagabonds. We end up being strangers wherever we go. And at least for me, an Internet community is no substitute for the real thing."

Sharing the Vision

After he worked with all six questions, the question that brought Ken to his vision was clearly, *Where do my family and I belong?* Invigorated by the question's potential to get them all out of their slumps, Ken set up a family discussion time. All four gathered around the kitchen table to strategize about their collective future. Everyone agreed that they didn't want to keep moving, that they wanted stability, even if—and this was a tough one for Ken—Ken's career might not advance as fast as it otherwise would.

The next natural question was, *Where?* They unanimously decided (with even young Morgan agreeing) that the Pacific Northwest did not feel like home to them. When they looked into their hearts, they felt drawn to the Southeast, where Ken and Mary Beth had both been raised and where the children had also spent their youngest years. It was decided: Ken would seek employment there within a year, as soon as it was practical to do so.

There and then, Ken and Mary Beth made a pact not to relocate the family again, at least until Adam and Morgan were both in college. Ken would confine his job search to areas within an hour's drive of high-tech centers, and they picked two areas everyone saw as livable, with decent weather and easy access to things they all loved, like the outdoors and parks. Finally, as an "insurance policy," Ken looked into the possibility of starting his own consulting firm. That way, if all else failed, he might be able to remain in the area instead of feeling obligated to go wherever his company might choose to send him. This new stability would also give the family an added benefit—Mary Beth would be able to restart her own career.

As with most quantum change, once the vision came together and the plan was set, the wheels set immediately into motion. Ken finished his project successfully and quickly took his leave on a high note. The family packed up the moving van for the last time and headed back east, to their chosen home. After they settled in and started putting down solid roots, Mary Beth looked into a re-

fresher course at the local medical college, with an eye toward a part-time job as a school nurse. Adam rebounded quickly, and he and Morgan thrived in their new home, making friends, getting involved in activities, keeping their parents very busy. The entire family could breathe easier and invest deeper, knowing they'd all made the commitment to stay put.

FINDING YOUR PLACE

The greater the distance we put between ourselves and the places we belong, the more frantic becomes our grasping for signposts and milestones that show us where we should live. These days, those signposts all point us to work—our functions in the economy have usurped every other sense of roots that we have.

It takes tremendous strength to resist the question *What is my position?*—every test we've taken, every promotion we've received encouraged us to rank ourselves according to others. ***Where do I belong?*** asks us to define our place by what we find inside, rather than what we see around us. Ralph Waldo Emerson tackled just this question in his treatise *Self-Reliance.*

> It is easy in the world to live after the world's opinion; it is easy in solitude to live after our own; but the great man is he who in the midst of the crowd keeps with perfect sweetness the independence of solitude.

Try to recapture this "perfect sweetness" as you contemplate the following exercises. Find a place where you can be alone for

15 minutes, and take out your journal. Spend five minutes answering the first set of questions and ten minutes answering the second.

- If you were meeting someone at a party and they asked "What do you do?" how would you answer? How would you identify your role in the social hierarchy or on the job?

- What are the words someone would use to describe you in that position—perhaps you are hard-working, efficient, thorough? What qualities do you need to perform that position well?

This lens of position is the question that most men and women find easiest to answer today—very simply, we are what we do and, in our minds, we *live* there, too.

- Now, think back on a time in your life when you were spending your time in a way that made you feel totally alive, like you belonged there—where are you and what are you doing? Describe this place, the people around you, the feeling of being connected to your passion—what was it about this place that made you feel so comfortable?

This second lens—the lens of belonging—offers a very different perspective on the world and our place in it. One of the differences between the first and second questions is who is benefiting most from your actions—is it you, or is it a larger entity or company? When we really belong somewhere, we always feel like we're getting the most out of our situation—whether we're earning millions of dollars for our company or tending to the wounds of the sick. When your heart is truly home, it will spill out of everything you do—you'll know that the feeling of belonging cannot be replaced by your position, no matter how prestigious it is or how much money it earns you. It just doesn't come close.

The Feeling of Coming Home

To a great extent, most of us believe that where we live is a matter of circumstance. Maybe that's where the jobs were, or where you got a great deal on a new house, or maybe where you grew up and never left. But whether school or work or family or serendipity drew you to your current home, it's crucial to see that where you live is always your choice. Is it truly where you belong?

One thing that amazes me about visionary experiences is when people tell me they have a definite sense of where they belong *even though they've never been there*. When they focus in on what their hearts are trying to tell them, they're able to conjure up a remarkably clear picture of the place that's right for them. I'm not sure why this happens, but my gut tells me that certain environments can either match or mismatch our temperaments, much like music, art, or our chosen work can. I have met people who knew they belonged in a bustling city without ever having lived in one and others who instinctively knew that the country was their destiny. They may have had only the slightest brush with an actual place, yet instantly know that's where they belong. The lasting impression is indelible. Take a few minutes to sit quietly and think of all the places you've ever lived or visited. Try to keep these images fresh in your mind as you answer the following questions.

- Can you recall ever having an experience like the one I mentioned above, a positive, visceral response to a place? Where were you? How old were you, and how did you get there? What were you doing there?

- When you daydream about being somewhere else, where does your mind take you? When you split this apart from the understandable need to take a vacation or get a break from your stressful job, is there any consistency in these daydreams? Do you tend, for example, to always daydream about the same place? What is that environment like?

- Think about your favorite books or movies—are they set in certain places? What might that say about where you yearn to be?

- Now, think about the place you currently live—is the lifestyle a good match for your personality and temperament? What do you like (or dislike) about the geography, the climate, the culture, the community? In what ways is it a good, or bad, match for you?

Aside from snarling about traffic jams and property taxes, we sometimes don't take the time to think about where we live in an abstract way. Use these questions to pull apart all the best and worst characteristics of your chosen place, and compare them to the traits of the places you loved to visit. What can you bring into your own life? What would you miss if you moved? What would you gain? Circle the words that speak most clearly to your sense of place, and save this information for when you later answer the six questions.

The Beauty of Belonging

Just as we are sometimes moved to become the people others think we ought to be, or try to substitute the pursuit of desires for the pursuit of meaning, so can we be tempted to build our identities and our self-esteem on our position. Tempting though it may be, this approach isn't good for our relationships, our children, or our souls. It is far better and more satisfying to root ourselves in where we belong and to balance that commitment with whatever positions we may hold as a way of anchoring ourselves in the world.

Chasing our fortunes around the countryside, we may try to compensate for our displacement by padding our nests—as foreign as they may feel—with material comforts. Yet the profound and comforting sense of personal security that comes from knowing where you belong has everything to do with the *people* that inhabit that place, not the *stuff*. The next question—***Whom do I love?***—will help us clearly define the difference between these two potent forms of attachment.

FOURTH QUESTION:

Whom Do I Love?

vs.

What Do I Own?

AGNES'S LOVE OF OTHERS
WAS HER DESTINY

Agnes's father was an Albanian grocer who would regale her with tales of local politics and other countries he visited on his wide travels. But in 1919, when she was nine, her beloved father unexpectedly died, leaving her mother to care for three children alone. Although the family had enjoyed a very comfortable living up until then, her mother was forced to take in sewing to make ends meet. Strong and equal to the task, Agnes's mother began crafting beautiful wedding dresses and intricate embroidery for some of the well-to-do women in the town. Despite her own difficulties, she also took time to care for other women in the neighborhood. When a nearby widow died, leaving six children, Agnes's mother took them in and raised them as her own.

The young Agnes respected her mother tremendously. She saw her dedication and resolved to adopt it. By the time she was twelve, in between studying, singing in the choir, and playing the mandolin, she began to suspect that she was being drawn to a life of service. After much thought, she still didn't know for certain what her true destiny was. "How does anyone know?" she asked her priest.

He told her, "The deep inner joy that you feel is the compass that indicates your direction in life."

She began her life of service as a nun teaching privileged students in India, but it was not until she was thirty-six that she heard her "call within a call." On September 10, 1946, while on a long train ride to Darjeeling, India, she experienced a burst of insight: Instead of being removed from the people who most needed her help, she would live among the people as she helped them, "to take care of the sick and the dying, the hungry, the naked, and the homeless—to be God's Love *in action* to the poorest of the poor." That day, she made plans to start her own religious order, the Missionaries of Charity. That woman became Nobel Prize–winning nun Mother Teresa.

Whom Do I Love?

*H*e Who Dies with the Most Toys, Wins. When I first saw this bumper sticker, I knew I was supposed to laugh, but it just struck me as incredibly cynical.

While this slogan came out of the go-go '80s—a time when many of us defined ourselves by our designer labels and the brand of bottled water we drank—the question *What do I own?* has never really gone away. Certainly, during the Internet boom economy of the 1990s, McMansions sprouted like mushrooms, with more and more square footage filled with the evidence that their owners had done everything right—chosen the right field, landed the right job, made the right investments. They had *arrived*.

To an extent, we all crave some fruits from our labor. In most of today's work, there's nothing tangible we can point to and say "I made that!" so we don't have the opportunity to savor a job well-done. Instead, we take our satisfaction from what we can buy, and these "toys" become the proof that we've played the game by the rules. Over time, those material things become our shorthand—I have things, so I must be worthy; without things, I'm nothing.

The fact that the entire economy and advertising industry are set up to aid and abet this human tendency only makes matters worse. When we feel underconfident or alone, commercials and billboards and magazine ads all scream out that forming a relationship with this car, this purse, this brand of toilet cleaner will make us feel whole and strong again. The average American receives thousands of these kinds of marketing messages every day, and by making our ethereal needs material, these goods give us something to hold on to. They may even temporarily fill those holes in our lives, only to disappoint when we realize that our problems remain the same, with or without this year's model.

Still, many of us, consciously or unconsciously, define a large portion of our lives by the question *What do I own?* What if we were instead to view our worldly attachments through an alternative lens, with the question **Whom do I love?** Asking this question can help us step off the consumption treadmill and put our attachment energy back into the relationships that really matter—with people, not products.

The following three stories show lives dominated by the lens of *What do I own?* First, we'll hear about how this question got these people into serious, often life-threatening situations; then we'll learn how **Whom do I love?** saved the ones who were willing to take the risk and open themselves up to caring. If your car ever sported the bumper sticker I mentioned above, there's still hope. What is attachment really about, anyway—your money? Or your life?

MIKE: HAVING IT ALL

Mike's firm grip struck me almost as much as his steady gaze did. He gave an impression of supreme confidence and total command, and his poised good looks and obvious wealth reminded me of Jay Gatsby, F. Scott Fitzgerald's charismatic creation. But like Gatsby's, Mike's carefully constructed façade soon revealed a hidden life.

Mike was in my office because—appearances aside—his life actually wasn't going that well. Mike had always liked to drink, and his wife, Alice, had made the appointment for him, saying she was very concerned about his recent drinking bouts. Early in their marriage, he drank a nightly cocktail plus expensive red wine with dinner. Now he was drinking cheap gin, which he'd buy by the case from a liquor store in a town where no one knew him. In addition to his weeknight benders, Mike was usually in the bag by two in the afternoon on weekends. His problem had only escalated since his recent promotion in his family's business, and Alice was afraid of where it would end up—it turns out, with very good reason.

Family Business

Alice had never really gotten the greatest feeling from Mike's father, a self-made millionaire who'd owned the largest, most successful corporation in the rural area where they lived. He was cool and aloof—his grandchildren shied away from him—but he was nothing compared to Mike's brusque mom. "His dad may be intimidating in his 'in-charge' way, but his mom was the really feared one," said Alice.

From the time they were small, Mike and his brother, Tom, had everything they could possibly want in the world—except love. Their parents expected them to work hard at boarding school and achieve in the classroom and on the athletic field. But the similarities between the two brothers ended at high-school graduation—while Mike went immediately into an executive role in the family business, Tom chose to go to law school instead. When Tom finished and passed the bar, he turned down his father's second lucrative offer—this time to be the corporation's attorney—to accept an entry-level job at an established law firm. Mike and his father thought Tom was nuts, but Tom clearly had a vision for his life, something his brother had not yet discovered.

Shortly after his thirtieth birthday, Mike was named chief operating officer, with his father retaining the titles of CEO, president, and primary shareholder. As part of his promotion, Mike was given twenty-five percent ownership of the company. By that time, between his salary and bonuses, he was already a rich man. He lived with Alice and his two young daughters in a fifteen-room house on one hundred and fifty acres of gently rolling hills, meadows, and streams. Their property also bordered on several hundred acres of protected old wood forest. Dirt roads were carved throughout the forest, and Mike loved to drive his Jeep deep into the woods during hunting season.

Mike loved to hunt, and he kept his substantial and expensive gun collection in a gun shed outside the house, in deference to Alice's discomfort with having them in the house. "Shed" was a misnomer, though—this small house adjoined the kennel of Mike's three prize hunting dogs and came complete with heat and air conditioning, a full bathroom, and even a small kitchen.

The shed was actually a big focus of Alice's worry and unhappiness. Lately, Mike had been spending a lot of time in there, away from her and the girls. Sometimes he wouldn't even stop in the house after work—he would just head directly to the shed. Between regular trips to the refrigerator, stocked exclusively with beer and liquor, Mike would spend hours loading shells, polishing his guns, and visiting with his dogs. When he wasn't in the shed, he'd go out cruising around the property in his Jeep.

Alice said it hadn't always been this way. When they met in college, she'd been attracted to the stability Mike offered, which was in stark contrast to her own family's financial struggles. But the more financially successful Mike became, the worse their relationship had become. Now she was beginning to see him as just a spoiled brat who indulged his every whim. "Personally, I don't think it makes him happy to own all these things," she said. "But he just keeps on spending." Mike's life held ample evidence of the maxim "Every increased possession loads us with a new weariness."

Even more troubling was Mike's decreasing interest in his two daughters. "About the only thing he still seems to enjoy is reading them a bedtime story now and then," she said. "But I can smell the gin on his breath and I'm sure they can, too. I'm just wondering how long it will be before one of them says something to him—and how he'll react."

Alice was desperate—she wanted to save her marriage before it slipped away—but the sad truth was that Mike was not ready to change. He denied that he had a drinking problem, putting the responsibility on his wife. "Alice doesn't like my drinking and she doesn't like my gun collection. She resents the money I spend on hunting trips—she doesn't even like the fact that I hunt at all," he said. "I think she'd like me to just come home every night and play games with the girls. But that's not the kind of man I am, and Alice just can't accept that." Mike had clearly come to view his life through the lens of *What do I own?*—a lens that blinded him to the people who loved him the most.

Mike decided not to come back to meet with me anymore, and I didn't hear from either of them for another year. When I finally did, I saw firsthand the sometimes-terrifying effects of turning

your back on the question ***Whom do I love?*** But first, let's hear two other stories.

BETH'S STORY: (NOT) WANTING ELEANOR'S THINGS

In contrast to Mike's embracing of his parents' lifestyle, Beth could not have cared less about her mother Eleanor's money. Beth's father had been a successful insurance and real-estate magnate who'd inherited a huge amount of money from his own father. By the time he died, at age seventy, he'd amassed a sizable fortune, much of which he left to Eleanor—and Eleanor clearly intended to hold on to every penny.

Eleanor and Martin were pushy and insistent parents who were *very* used to getting their way. With influences this dominant, it had not been easy for Beth to follow her own path, but she had— she'd gone to college and studied library science, and she now worked as the head librarian for her town. Bright, straightforward, and tirelessly cheerful, Beth loved teaching the local kids and high-school students how to use the library. Her husband, Tyler, had graduated from an Ivy League law school, and became a public defender instead of taking a more lucrative position in a private firm. Beth's parents couldn't get enough of ridiculing him for this choice—when Beth and Tyler struggled financially, her parents had sarcastically suggested to her that things would be fine if Tyler "would just smell the coffee and get a real job."

With their combined salaries, Beth and Tyler's family enjoyed a comfortable but not extravagant lifestyle, unlike the way her parents lived. Raised in lavish surroundings, Beth and her siblings had looked on while their parents spent great sums on artwork and entertaining, yet remained almost cruelly stingy when it came to their own kids. In retrospect, Beth saw this as more of a blessing than a curse—it had left her with no craving for luxury and no extravagant expectations for what life ought to be like.

Her siblings felt the same way—although they were slightly more bitter about their parents' neglect and abuse. In place of affection, Eleanor and Martin had showered their children with a constant barrage of criticism that gave each of them the nagging feeling that they'd never measure up. As a result, each built up an armor of resentment and dropped out of their parents' lives—all except Beth, whose self-esteem remained strong, probably from staying true to her own vision and falling in love with a man who did the same.

The widow Eleanor was quite content with her distant relationships. Her children's estrangement may never have become an issue if she hadn't, as we all eventually do, grown old.

A Different Set of Values

Seventy-five-year-old Eleanor's body was breaking down. Increasingly infirm, she resisted any help, but Beth knew that she and her siblings needed to do something. True to form, Eleanor rejected both a full-time live-in companion and a move to an assisted living center. She continued to live alone, and her only regular visits—aside from Beth's—were from the cleaning lady who came in once a week. The mansion choked with fine art, statues, and expensive antiques—all of which were well-dusted but rarely seen—and slowly fell into a state of disrepair from a lack of basic maintenance.

From her bed, Eleanor would bark out bitterly that her children were scavengers, waiting for her to die so they could inherit the family wealth. Not surprisingly, Eleanor's few callers dwindled to one—Beth—and even her visits had grown fewer and shorter. In an effort to deal with this obviously painful situation, Beth brought her sister and brother to my office so the three could talk about options for Eleanor. During that meeting, I started to realize just how much Eleanor had identified herself with her wealth and social position instead of her own children.

None of her children felt attached to their mother—in fact, if it weren't for Beth, the others would probably have avoided her altogether. "Mother truly believes that we love her money more than we love her, but I think that's the way *she* feels about us," Martin Jr. said. "For as long as I can remember, she's always acted as if the furniture, the artwork, even her damn jewelry were more valuable than any of us."

Beth's sister, Margaret, agreed. "I've always believed that mother would grieve more if the house burned down, or if her precious art collection was stolen, than if all three of us died in a car accident," she said.

Eleanor had so clearly identified with *What do I own?* that she probably would've viewed the question **Whom do I love?** as horrifyingly sentimental. Thankfully, she got one more chance to redeem herself before her children, Beth included, gave up on her completely. But let's first hear about Doug and Heidi.

DOUG AND HEIDI'S STORY: TOYS WERE COMING BETWEEN THEM

Doug lived to play. One year, he bought three mountain bikes—one of them was particularly high-tech and cost well over a thousand dollars. He also owned five kayaks, a motorcycle, and an all-terrain vehicle. He and his wife, Heidi, had had to build a barn to house his ever-growing collection of toys—but the catch was, Heidi never got to play with them. She wasn't in the kind of physical shape that would allow her to keep up with Doug, and he had no intention of slowing down to help her.

Initially, Heidi thought that her biggest complaint was that Doug would buy his "toys"—even the expensive items—without discussing them with her first. They'd been married twelve years, and although they weren't wealthy, they were hardly uncomfortable. They had no children and enjoyed the luxury of plenty of disposable income, but in all this "fun," their marriage was slowly breaking down.

"At first I really liked Doug's ability to cut loose—it was so different from my dad, who had always been a workaholic," she said. "But in choosing Doug, I've come to think I went to the opposite extreme. I think I expected that Doug would change after we got married and as we got older. But the only thing that's changed has been how much money and time he spends on his toys."

Heidi's biggest complaint wasn't that he had the toys, but where he chose to use them—far away from her. She was afraid that whatever relationship they'd once had was now being subsumed by his passion for outdoor sports. "He spends a major amount of time either with friends or by himself," she said. "Sometimes I wonder if he's more attached to some of his gear than he is to me."

Doug had clearly heard all this before, but instead of focusing on Heidi's feelings of being abandoned, Doug chose to focus on the money question. "I've never asked Heidi to account for the way she spends her money, so I don't see any reason why I should have to," he said, in a measured response that suggested he'd delivered it before. The two had agreed to divide the household bills and other living expenses, and as long as he was living up to his end, he didn't see any reason why he should "report" to Heidi about how he spent the rest of his money. It was the clash of the two questions—Heidi was hoping Doug would ask, **Whom do I love?** Instead, he thought she wanted him to ask, *What do I own?*

As the two sat in front of me, arms crossed and looking in opposite directions, I saw two people who were at a crossroads in their relationship. For Doug, the relationship was perfectly okay, aside from Heidi's carping. He said that he was willing to take her with him on his outdoor adventures—but when asked if that meant he would adjust his pace so that Heidi could keep up, he hesitated, and she laughed. "I don't think that's really an option," she said. He didn't disagree.

The way Doug wanted to structure their relationship didn't impress Heidi as being much of a relationship at all. "There's so little 'we' in our marriage," she said. "I always believed we'd grow closer together as time passed, but we're two people leading separate lives under one roof. It makes me wonder why we bother staying together." She sighed and turned to Doug. "I mean, what's the point?"

LOVING PEOPLE, PLACES, AND THINGS

Stories like these are more common than you might think. Mike, Eleanor, and Doug had all chosen, consciously or unconsciously, to embrace things more passionately than people. Their lives were a testament to acquisitiveness. All of them, I was sure, would have no trouble compiling lengthy inventories in response to the question *What do I own?*

Why would people choose to attach themselves so much to *things*? Human nature is partially to blame. Starting from when we are very young, most of us form emotional bonds, not only to people, but to places and things—our childhood homes, for example, or a favorite sweater. As we grow older, the most important question is one of balance: How even are our attachments?

Your Attachment Inventory

Your attachment inventory will help you trace the development of your attachments from childhood to the present. Take out your journal and copy the form below onto a full page.

Childhood Attachments

People I was attached to:

_____

_____

_____

Places I was attached to:

_____

_____

_____

Things I was attached to:

_____

_____

_____

Attachments are really all about *nouns*: people, places, and things. Take fifteen to twenty minutes to really think about the answers to these questions. You'll use the answers for these exercises at the end of the chapter.

- First, who were the *people* you were closest to? Most of us would cite one or both of our parents, but you could also include a grandparent, a kind neighbor, or an older sibling who played a central role in your life. Who made you feel most safe and loved?

- *Places* also play an important role in our childhoods. Where did you feel the most safe and connected? Was it a tree house, your bedroom closet, your grandmother's front porch?

- Finally, think of the *things* you were attached to as a child. Children are notorious for forming close ties to stuffed animals, dolls, or blankets. Even the famous Orson Welles character, Charles Foster Kane from *Citizen Kane*, was so attached to his beloved sled Rosebud that it was literally the last word he uttered on his deathbed.

Emerson said, "Great men are they who see that spiritual is stronger than any material force, that thoughts rule the world." *Sure*, you think, *in an ideal world, maybe*. The fact is, it's human nature to want things and even to feel attached to them, but we need a balance between material interests and spirituality to be psychologically healthy. When *What do I own?* dominates our worldview, it sends us looking outward, leading us to greed, egocentrism, and selfishness; it narrows our lives and isolates us from other people. When we define ourselves by *What do I own?* we're essentially saying, "I am what I possess."

In contrast, **Whom do I love?** inspires us to look inward, into our hearts, to find the answer. We replace egotism with altruism, caring as much about our beloved as we do about ourselves. Powerful, life-changing visions have been triggered by this simple question, three of which you'll read about now.

DOUG AND HEIDI: MAKING CHANGES

As defensive as Doug was about his habits, when Heidi questioned the future of their relationship, he was startled. He obviously hadn't thought things were that bad. He offered, "Maybe we can spend more time together. If you'd like to plan something, let me know and I'll arrange my schedule to be there."

This halfhearted proposal turned into several weekend afternoons together—more time than Heidi and Doug had devoted to their relationship in years. Heidi was overjoyed—she'd waited a long time to reconnect with Doug. But despite this slow and steady progress, I still got the sense that Doug was placating Heidi and killing time rather than acting out of genuine interest.

One week, Heidi caught the flu—or at least that's what they thought it was. When it wouldn't go away, Heidi went to the doctor, who ordered some tests. Before Doug and Heidi could catch their breath, the doctors had her diagnosis: Heidi had leukemia.

Shocked into immediate action, the two committed themselves fully to Heidi's recovery. Her treatment would last for months and would sap both her physical and her emotional reserves. While the doctors were optimistic and the progress reports were good, it didn't really stop her or Doug from worrying as she headed into the most intense part of her treatment.

Watching over Heidi as she received an IV drip of chemotherapy while she dozed, Doug had a moment of awakening: He realized that he'd never imagined they'd get sick or even grow old. "I've always thought of myself, and Heidi, too, as being twenty-one years old forever," he said. He saw that Heidi was right—they had been drifting away from each other, and he admitted to himself that his penchant for to play and fun may have been part of the problem.

"It wasn't until Heidi got sick that I realized just how much I really do love her," he said. "I immediately recognized how attached I was to her, and how devastated I would be if anything ever happened to her."

Heidi's illness had shocked Doug out of his formerly limited worldview, a never-never land where no one ever got sick or grew old. Her treatment was successful, and the effects it had on their relationship were equally transformative. For Doug, life gained a depth it had lacked before. Although he was still involved in his outdoor activities, he now had balance. "I feel blessed to have the best of both worlds—adventure and a good relationship," he said. "These days I don't take anything for granted, which makes life much more interesting."

The prospect of losing Heidi showed him very quickly how hollow the question *What do I own?* was when compared to **Whom do I love?** Doug saw this shift as a blessing that helped make his life richer and more resonant. Put simply, in those very intense few months, Doug finally grew up.

BETH AND ELEANOR: IT'S NEVER TOO LATE

Although none of Beth's siblings believed it was possible, Eleanor's declining health continued to sour her disposition even more. Her three children wanted to do what was morally right for her, but they also needed to know that it would be endurable for *them*. After many talks, only Beth still wanted to continue having regular contact with her mother. She'd admitted to herself that expecting her mother's love and approval would just set her up for disappointment. Instead, Beth made peace with her decision to visit for her *own* needs—she wanted to ensure that after her mother was gone, she would know she'd done the right thing for herself, instead of giving in to anger and resentment.

By lowering her expectations, and with support from her siblings, Beth was able to insulate herself from her mother's rage. Still, it wasn't easy. In the span of six months, two helpers quit, saying frankly that they weren't paid enough to put up with Eleanor's nastiness.

Shortly after the second one quit, Eleanor broke her hip in a fall and was hospitalized. During her stay, dutiful Beth came to check in and see how she was feeling. While Beth sat next to her mother's bed, trying to make conversation, her mother muttered that she was sure one of her children would sneak into the house and steal her paintings while she was in the hospital.

"Normally a comment like this would send me through the roof," Beth recalled. "But this time, I just looked her straight in the eye and told her the truth: 'Mother, nobody wants your paintings. We never have. We only wanted your love, but we gave up on that a long time ago.'"

With that, she gathered her purse and coat and turned to go. With her back to her mother's bed, she said, "And if you're wondering what I'm doing here, it's so I can look at myself in the mirror after you're gone and say I did right by you, even if you never loved me." Beth closed the door behind her without a backward glance.

It took Beth a while before she could make herself go to visit her mother again. She waited until her mother was sent home from the hospital, and then dropped by briefly—she wasn't about to force herself to linger or chat. She couldn't be sure, but Beth thought she noticed a change in her mom—she wasn't being what anyone would call "nice," but the cutting harshness was definitely diminished. After a strained half-hour, Beth was about to say a quick good-bye when she did a double take—was her mother crying? "I'd never even seen a tear in my mother's eye, and it definitely made me uncomfortable," Beth said. She mumbled that she'd be back soon and hurried out the door.

After seventy-five years of asking *What do I own?* could it be that Eleanor had finally decided to ask herself **Whom do I love?** That question had basically cracked open the shell that had surrounded her heart and led to a vision—she realized, in one quick, painful second, that her children had all but given up on her love. When this epiphany was combined with the sudden, clear truth of Beth's real motivation—love, not greed—Eleanor was forced to see beyond her own limited worldview of money and possessions. She looked into her own heart, and to her surprise, she discovered love there.

Slowly, tentatively, Eleanor tried on the cloak of the loving mother and doting grandmother. Coaxed by Beth's enthusiastic tales, the other siblings followed suit, brought their children over, and began to see that their mother *really* had changed. Thankfully, her children were eager to forgive and enjoyed, for the first time, a rich and rewarding relationship with their mom.

We can say "Better late than never," but if we're honest, Eleanor's vision and quantum change came *very* close to being too late. Perhaps in recognition of her own mortality, Eleanor's transformation into a caring mother and loving grandmother was immediate and dramatic, but think of all those years the family lost out on!

MIKE AND ALICE: FALLOUT

About a year after my only meeting with Mike, Alice called me—she needed to see me right away. It was then that I learned what dangerous fallout could result from clinging to *What do I own?*

When we met, she quickly caught me up on the family's story. After our last meeting, Mike had promised to cut down on his drinking, but that didn't last long—he slid from Cabernet with dinner back to cheap gin and vodka in a mere three weeks. Alice all but gave up and started going to Al-Anon to deal with the torment of the situation. Then, Mike's father had begun discussing retiring and appointing Mike as CEO within the next twelve months. Rather than exciting Mike, this revelation seemed to send him into a deeper funk—he started drinking more and stopped coming into the house except to sleep. And then there'd been an accident.

Mike was fond of driving around his property in his Jeep with the top off. One afternoon, soon after Alice had left for a baby shower, Mike blew into the kitchen in the midst of his daughters' afternoon snack and asked if they wanted to take a ride with Daddy through the woods. Naturally, they jumped at the chance. The nanny could smell liquor on Mike's breath, so she distracted the girls with cookies while she tried to change Mike's mind. She attempted to reason with him, saying that they should finish their snack and then go for a swim, but Mike just waved her off dismissively. When she protested more vigorously, he barked at her, took the girls, and stormed out of the house.

The nanny watched nervously from the window as he took off down the back lawn with the kids, not one of them wearing a seat belt. They hadn't driven more than a hundred yards when Mike sideswiped a tree and lost control of the steering wheel. The Jeep lurched to one side, hit a ditch, and drove straight through a short hedge, which stopped the vehicle's forward momentum. Mike collided with the steering wheel, and both girls were thrown out of the nanny's line of sight.

The nanny sprinted out of the house, down the back lawn. Simultaneously, the groundskeeper stopped his tractor, ran to his truck, and sped off in the direction of the crash, pausing only long enough for the nanny to jump in. She barely waited for the truck to stop before she sprang out and ran into the hole in the hedge. Sheer luck or divine intervention had fixed it so the girls had landed safely in a patch of tall grass, just inches from a stone wall. If their father had been driving just a little faster, this story would have a completely different ending. As it was, they were scratched up and emotionally traumatized, but neither of them had suffered serious physical injury.

The nanny scooped up the girls and whisked them back to the truck. The groundskeeper put his hand on Mike's shoulder, but Mike was looking down at the ground, dazed. He waved them off, and the groundskeeper hopped in the truck and hit the gas. As they surged forward, the nanny saw Mike out of the corner of her eye, wandering in the same tall grass that had spared his daughters' lives.

When Alice got home, she immediately sensed that something was wrong. She found Mike in the kitchen, bruised face in his hands. "Where are they?" she demanded.

"At the hospital," Mike croaked. Alice turned on her heels and was gone.

Making Changes

Alice didn't speak to Mike at all the first week after the accident. "Truthfully, it was all I could do to be in the same house with him," she said. "When we finally spoke, I asked him to talk to someone or go to AA. He hasn't done either, so it won't be long until he gets over his fear and starts to drink again."

Alice was committed to her Al-Anon meetings, where she bonded with kindred souls who'd endured many of the same trials she had. Inspired by the discussions there, she wondered if she should take some time to delve into her past, to think about the "personality flaw" that would attract her to someone like Mike. To me, this seemed like wasted effort, focusing so intensely on something that happened long in the past. "Couldn't it be that you were just attracted to the Mike you knew in college, before you knew he was an alcoholic?" I asked her.

Alice was eager to look forward instead of back, and she realized that she had wasted enough time waiting for Mike to come around. That's when she began her own journey of self-exploration, working with the six questions. Over the next few months, Alice began to develop her own vision, especially when she hit upon the question **Whom do I love?** She realized that she'd always craved the material security that Mike's family afforded—thinking in terms of *What do I own?*—but now the life she had with Mike did not feel secure. On the contrary, she was living in constant fear that the worst could happen at any moment. The accident had also underscored her love for her children, but Alice was forced to admit that she no longer felt the same way about Mike. In place of the love she once felt were feelings of concern, nostalgia, and a healthy dose of anger that just wouldn't go away—but no love.

Life on the estate did not feel like home. She'd wanted to be sheltered, but the image that came to her from the question **Where do I belong?** was less isolated and more cozy than the gigantic mansion she'd been rattling around in for the past ten years. To her, their house was a symbol of Mike's position in life, but it wasn't where she *belonged.*

The crowning piece of Alice's vision fell into place when she asked herself **Why am I here?** and realized that she wanted to pick up her original career plan, the one she'd abandoned when she and Mike first met. He had always been opposed to the idea of Alice working. ("Why should you work?" he'd say. "I make plent, ᴏɪ money. Don't you think it's more important for you to be with the girls?") Though she'd allowed herself to be persuaded (or *bullied*) by Mike's arguments, the idea of turning her back on her dreams had never really set well with Alice. She recalled her first ambition—to become a CPA—and that goal was the jump start to Alice's life change.

Once her vision came together, Alice's quantum change began with a bang. A year and a half after the car accident, Alice and her girls were living in a snug, warm house within easy driving distance of Alice's family. She was working and going to school part time to earn an MBA in accounting, and she had a long-term goal of either starting her own business or joining a small firm. She was content, and felt safe, at last.

Mike still saw the girls every couple of weeks. He was careful never to show up with alcohol on his breath, but Alice knew he was still drinking—at that point, what did he have to lose? Sadly, Mike never got over his anger. The hardest part for him was coming to terms with the fact that his money couldn't keep his family with him. Mike's insistence on seeing his life through the lens of *What do I own?* held him back from perhaps the one thing that could've saved him—the love of his family.

OUR SEARCH FOR LOVE

These dramatic stories prove that the seemingly innocuous question *What do I own?* can pack a life-threatening punch. For the moment, put aside all thoughts of money or possessions—the true root of any issue with attachment to *things* is the quality of our attachment to *people*, the matter we'll delve into here. Turn to a fresh page in your journal, and set aside 20 minutes to answer the following questions. If any of the questions bring up emotions you haven't thought about in a while, circle those answers—you can flip back to them when you answer your six questions.

- Take a look at your attachment inventory (see "Your Attachment Inventory" on page 122). Among the people you were closest to, do you recall ever experiencing any painful separations from these people? Were these relationships consistently loving and supportive, or did you sometimes feel abused or betrayed? Write down the specifics: When was this? How old were you? Did the situation resolve itself? Are there people in your life now with whom you feel similar emotions? (Experiences like these can breed insecurity and mistrust and make it more difficult to be generous with your love. Recognizing these traits can lead you to a new vision of how you want to love others, a way of loving that's not controlled by your past.)

- Who was your first love? What was his or her name? What happened to this relationship? If it ended (as most first loves do), did it leave any lasting scars? Can you look back on this person now and enjoy a warm memory? If not, why? Write a list of the good and bad characteristics of that relationship—which ones have followed you into your current relationship patterns? Which would you like to keep? Which would you like to be rid of, finally and forever? What can you learn to inform your new vision of love? Circle the words that you feel represent both the very best and the very worst characteristics of all close relationships.

- Make a list of all the people you love now, from the one you love most to those you love less intensely. For each person on your list, write down a description of how you express your love for them: Do you spend time really listening to your mom? Do you go to your kids' soccer games? Do you shower your spouse with tender care when he or she is sick? Be specific. How often do you tell each of these people directly that you love them? Look at this list with pride—these attachments are your *true* accomplishments.

Grounded Relationships in a Shifting World

When we grant our possessions the same kind of devotion normally reserved for our loved ones, these objects take on the power to destroy our ties to the very people who can save us. It would serve us well to always remember that a main goal of a consumer economy is to find the customer's insecurities and exploit them for all they're worth. The next time you're tempted to put all your happiness eggs into a nest overflowing with things, ask yourself the question *Whom do I love?*—this lampshade, or my lover?

In this cold, alienating world, true reassurance of love and acceptance can be a tough thing to come by. Even if we've licked the materialism monster, there's a flip side that can draw us in. The same market economy that seeks to seduce us into *purchasing* things to prove our worth also works in reverse—it plays upon our need to please others by driving us to diligently *produce* things. As a result, many of us try desperately to prove our worth by serving other people's needs. Oprah Winfrey has called this drive "the disease to please." We'll tackle this scourge as we answer the question *Who loves me?*

FIFTH QUESTION:

Who Loves Me?

vs.

What Am I Worth?

ANNA BECAME
LOVED BY MILLIONS

Anna was born five years before the start of the Civil War and grew up on her parents' farm, working hard at her chores and receiving schooling only briefly during the summers. As a child, she loved to draw pictures and color them with the juice of berries and grapes—she called them her "lambscapes."

But farm life didn't allow much time to dally with creative pursuits. At age twelve, Anna left home to work as a hired girl on another family's farm, beginning what she referred to as "the hard years." She cooked and weeded and hoed the garden, working steadily as a loyal and valued employee to others, until she met Thomas, also a hired hand on the farm. When they married, Anna was twenty-seven.

The two set off on a grand adventure, moving to a warmer climate and buying a small farm of one hundred acres, dishes, cows, and all. Together, they worked the farm and raised their family. Anna gave birth to ten babies there, but only five of them lived past infancy. Her days were filled with the arduous work of a farm wife: milking cows, making clothes, putting up produce for the winter. Her homemade jellies, pies, and canned goods earned her ribbons at the county fair. When her advancing age forced her to stop working so hard, she took up embroidery. Soon her debilitating arthritis made that too painful, so her sister Celestia suggested painting instead.

In the past, Anna had restricted her painting to little pictures made as Christmas presents because Thomas had considered her painting foolish. But one night, just weeks before he died, he pointed to one of her paintings and said, "That's really good." In his last remaining weeks, he insisted that she paint for him while he watched over her shoulder.

By the time she died at 101, she had produced two thousand paintings, most of them on Masonite board. Those paintings garnered her international acclaim. The work of legendary folk artist Grandma Moses still hangs in some of the most prestigious museums in the world.

Who Loves Me?

Groucho Marx is not typically seen as one of the pillars of august philosophy. But this cigar-chomping, sibling-abusing crank summed up one of our most debilitating habits in a keenly insightful joke: "I don't care to belong to any club that will accept me as a member."

It's funny because it's all too painfully true. When we don't value our worth as human beings, we become trapped in this contradiction: If other people treat us better than we think we deserve, we assume they're not to be trusted, so we reject them. But we don't exactly walk around proclaiming this complicated rationale to the world—we hide our insecurity, masking it with sarcasm or aloof coolness or a "you-can't-touch-me" demeanor. We treat Thomas Paine's words like gospel: "What we obtain too cheap, we esteem too lightly; it is dearness only that gives everything its value." As a species, we are hooked on playing hard to get.

Inside, though, those of us who have trouble believing in our own value live in constant fear of being found out for the "frauds" that we are. We trust the people who mistreat us because they can obviously see what these other, more easily duped people cannot—that we are not worthy of love. When true love comes around, it seems like a suspicious interloper, a ticking time bomb certain to explode in our faces if we ever open up. We keep our barriers up, waiting, waiting—in the meantime, we embrace the "love" we recognize all too well: criticism, abuse, a fundamental lack of caring.

Does this sound familiar? Maybe you've watched as a friend continues to fall in love with men who disrespect her, or you've commiserated with the guy who breaks his back trying to fulfill his wife's demands. Okay, now let's be honest—how many of these people are actually ourselves? Why do we get involved with the very people who will never grant us love? Perhaps a better question is, Why don't we see the value in the love we've been given by those worthy of *us*?

When we don't listen to and honor our truest selves, we leave it to others to define us. We ask *What am I worth?* while running the numbers in our heads, trying to measure our value to others and to society. We bend over backward trying to prove we are the good friend, worker, mother, lover, looking for that reassurance in the eyes of others. We say, "Here, I've done this for you—is it enough?" but when the answer is "Yes," we don't believe it—and the cycle begins again. It is possible to escape this endless loop, however. Instead of clinging to the constant measurement of *What am I worth?* we can break out of this trap with one very simple question: **Who loves me?**

Self-esteem experts often say we need to build skills to feel strong—set goals, master them, and *then* you'll feel good about yourself, they say. But what happens if you work and strive and achieve, and still you don't feel loved? You might feel proud of yourself, but you're still bound to be pretty darn lonely. All the career success in the world can't buy the feeling of being loved and valued simply for being yourself.

Who loves me? helps us begin to identify those people who need no proof that we're worth their time, the people who love us exactly the way we are, *as is.* These people hold tremendous potential for healing; they teach us that we can be loved regardless of what we believe are our faults or flaws—indeed, maybe even because of them. Their confidence and faith can give us the shelter and comfort we need to grow strong. The more we can surround ourselves with people who truly love us, and the less time we spend with people who make us question our own worth, the more likely we are to embrace our visions and quantum change. Carl and Eileen both found that the question **Who loves me?** was the key to their life-changing visions.

CARL'S STORY: THE VALUE OF WORK

Carl was a bear of a man, tall and stocky, but muscular. Perhaps it was his brute strength that had helped him survive his violent childhood. His father was an overbearing and hostile man who beat and verbally abused his wife and sons on a regular basis. When Carl was five, his father left and never came back. Perhaps it was for the best.

Carl's mother's chronic depression prevented her from keeping jobs for very long. Often, the family had to depend on welfare and charity to survive. Carl remembered many a Thanksgiving dinner spent in a church basement as guests of the Salvation Army. They moved often, hopping between cheap motels where Carl's mother would cook makeshift meals on a hot plate that traveled with them. They'd stay until the management kicked them out, either for not paying or for creating a safety hazard.

Carl's older brother had absorbed a lot of anger from his father, anger that found a ready target on Carl's tender skin. "I was a walking bruise," said Carl. "I cannot tell you how many social workers showed up at our door. Of course, my mother and I would cover up for my brother. After they left, she'd yell at him, but he just ignored her."

Since she couldn't control his brother, Carl's mom asked her sisters to take in young Carl, completely against his wishes. Each time he was brought to his aunts' house, he took the first opportunity to run away and return home. One time, his mother had moved to another motel in the interim; he found her only by hitching rides and walking for miles, from one motel to another. Finally, Human Services caught wind of the seriousness of Carl's situation. Just after his twelfth birthday, Carl's mother was charged with neglect and he was packed off to a residential facility. Again he bolted, but this time, when he showed up at his mother's door, the authorities were waiting to take him back to school.

"Something inside me just snapped—I could almost feel it," he said. "That was the last time I tried to run. I went back to the institution and stayed there. My mother visited me every so often, and I went home for Christmas one time, but it was awful." He thought they would have a nice holiday together; instead, his brother beat him senseless.

That visit was a turning point for Carl. When he got back to school, he made a decision to channel his energy into becoming independent instead of trying to get back home. He was tired of the abuse. He also finally realized that his mother wasn't capable of controlling his brother or creating a stable life for them.

Without knowing it, Carl had just defined his first vision. From that moment on, he felt energized and optimistic, and his formerly dismal life took an entirely different direction. He turned his back on his self-defeating obsession with getting back home and applied that stubborn will to creating his own life.

More than anything else, Carl wanted to be self-sufficient. He wanted to be able to support himself and create a life of stability, security, and comfort instead of the chaos and abuse he'd known as a child. From the moment he decided to accept his situation rather than fight it, he pursued his new vision with dogged determination.

Carl had decided to make his life mean something, so he wanted every second to count in his progress toward his goals. He set about becoming a star student, and despite his own tragic background, he became a mentor to other boys and helped them replace chronic failure with their first taste of success. That experience earned him a scholarship to study education in college; he then went on to graduate school and developed a distinguished career as a teacher who worked with socially and emotionally maladjusted students. By all accounts, he'd achieved way more than the independence he'd sought as an abandoned twelve-year-old boy. So why was he so miserable?

The Myth of the Midlife Crisis

When Carl came into my office, his first words to me were, "I'm having a midlife crisis."

Then he laughed and said, "I know that probably sounds clichéd, but that captures how I'm feeling." He'd just passed forty, and lately, he'd begun to think his life hadn't been a success. "Frankly, when I look at myself in the mirror in the morning, I don't like what I see. It's not just because I'm out of shape—it goes much deeper."

Objectively, Carl had been very successful at pursuing his early vision—he had a career, a family, and a home. He was not dependent on anyone, and he had never seen a welfare check in his life. He still made a habit of volunteering at a local soup kitchen on Thanksgiving. But although Carl had risen from the ashes and become a success, his lifestyle wasn't balanced. He joked that he was a workaholic, a sentiment that he said was echoed by his wife and thirteen-year-old daughter. I remarked to Carl that his daughter was about the same age that he'd been when he had his first vision. "Maybe she's ripe for her own vision," I said. He looked startled by the idea. "And maybe you are again, too," I added.

As Carl worked through each of the six questions, he was very grateful and appreciative to realize that he had some great answers, especially for the first three. A career in teaching had been a satisfying answer for *Who am I?* and a good fit with his personality and interests. Teaching had also answered the second question—*Why am I here?*—by infusing purpose and meaning in his life. When he asked *Where do I belong?* he realized that he felt a strong sense of place in both his classroom and his garden. All of these positive answers stemmed directly from the strength of Carl's first vision, which had pointed the way for him since adolescence.

Over the years, Carl had received numerous awards, including being named teacher of the year twice. When he asked the question *Whom do I love?* his students were clearly a part of the answer. He was constantly getting letters from grateful former students and praise from happy parents. A number of ex-students stayed in close contact with him, by mail, by phone, or via e-mail. The downside to these strong connections was the time it took to honor all his commitments—Carl worked a tremendous number of hours, and most days he could be found at his desk well after his colleagues had left. He worked at home, too, correcting papers and fine-tuning the next day's lessons. Over the summer, he developed curricula in his field and taught a college course in special education to earn extra money.

When I asked Carl how much time he spent with his family, he seemed caught off guard. "I'm home every night," he replied, but that wasn't exactly an answer to my question. We sat in silence for a few moments while he thought. Then he spoke, quietly and openly.

"Work is definitely a big part of my self-esteem. It always has been, ever since I was a teenager. It's what I do best," he said. "In fact, I'd say hard work saved my life." The last sentence hung in the air between us, and Carl looked away.

Then his face lit up. "That's it!" he said. Hearing himself say "Work saved my life" sparked what would develop into a new vision for Carl. In that one moment, he saw with total clarity how he had devoted his entire teenage and adult life to building what boiled down to his *résumé*. With his long line of accomplishments and obvious contributions to the lives of students, parents, and colleagues, he'd become very good at answering the question *What am I worth?* But now he wanted to know what was beyond that.

The Vision That Ran Its Course

The phrase *midlife crisis* has been tossed around for so long, no one really has any idea what it means. While many people talk about a sense of feeling lost inside their own lives, truthfully, these crises can be as different as the individuals who experience them. Some people seem to be casting about for a vision; others seem like they've had one, but lost the nerve to follow it up.

Carl's case was different still—the revelation that he'd had as a teen had served him well for many years and had probably even saved his life. But now, even though Carl was a successful man who had followed his dreams, he was still troubled and depressed. Did it mean that Carl needed to achieve more work-related success? How many awards and testimonials did he need to prove he'd done a good job? No, there was something else going on here.

Carl's life had turned out dramatically differently from his mother's and brother's lives. His mom had never conquered her depression, remaining on the fringes of society until her death ten years before. His brother, whom he hadn't seen since her funeral, had become a repeat offender who drifted in and out of jail. Carl could easily spend a while plumbing the depths of his childhood, but what he really needed was to recapture the vigor and energy he'd drawn from his vision at twelve years old. Now, almost three decades later, it was time for a new vision—the first had run its course.

Not surprisingly, when he recognized this, Carl felt a certain emptiness, almost as if a best friend or soulmate had died. The organizing principle that had kept him company through his loneliest days—to be independent and successful—was no longer serving his needs. Carl's life had stalled in large part because several of its major themes were out of balance. When it came to answering **Whom do I love?** for example, Carl seemed to be choosing his garden and his students over his family. He was more involved with some of his former students, whom he knew from a distance, than he was with his wife and daughter, with whom he shared a house. He spent far more time tending to his garden than he did tending to his family. And when it came to the value he placed on himself, Carl had focused much of his energy on answering the question *What am I worth?* while ignoring the more sustaining question **Who loves me?**

Answering the Love Question

Carl obviously had a very hard time letting himself be loved. But how could someone who was clearly loved and adored by so many be so closed to accepting their love and affection?

Carl knew that his daughter, Hannah, was an excellent student, but he sheepishly admitted that he generally didn't know anything about her homework assignments or even the names of her teachers. Although she'd been playing soccer for years, he'd rarely attended games and wasn't sure if the team had a winning or losing record. He also didn't know the names of the physicians in the office where his wife had worked for ten years.

Such a devoted teacher knew so little about what his own daughter studied in school. The initial explanation for this had a lot to do with the traumas Carl had endured as a child. The effects of his separation from his mother, his father's desertion, his brother's abuse, and the experience of being wrenched from the family, had all combined to make it hard for him to get close to others. No wonder his self-esteem was founded on work and achievement, which were completely under his control. In the worldview Carl had formed as a child, the people you love most, hurt you most.

Looking Forward

When I asked who loved him, he quickly answered, "Jeanne and Hannah," but the question itself made Carl squirm in his chair. He told me that he'd always been called detached, but that he prided himself on being an intellectual person. "I'm not one of those touchy-feely types," he said. This distinction was pretty handy for Carl—if the world were separated into thinkers and feelers, he'd chosen his camp, making it very easy for him to divorce himself from his emotions. But now that he was confronting it head-on, he had to admit that this distance had played a large part in the increasing estrangement in his marriage.

As is true for all couples, Jeanne and Carl had established well-worn patterns in their relationship. Their marriage had survived on very little intimacy and communication—Jeanne had learned long ago that she would have to build her own life based on close friendships and activities that could fill the time she wasn't spending with Carl. Consequently, when Carl decided he was ready to invest more in their relationship, it wasn't that easy for Jeanne to just turn back—she didn't want to resist him, but she had some lingering resentment. Luckily, even though Carl was out of practice and his overtures to Jeanne were awkward, she could see the beautiful man she loved trying his hardest and decided to give him another chance.

In the growing warmth between them, Jeanne was able to unburden herself of a fear she'd had for months: She suspected that Hannah had an eating disorder. When their daughter was under stress, facing deadlines or league playoffs, she would pig out and eat everything in sight, usually in hiding; yet at other times, it was as if she was on a starvation diet. She was also becoming obsessed with exercise. The revelation left Carl devastated—he felt guilty for not recognizing it before, and he didn't have the first idea how he could handle it. With all of his professional expertise, he wasn't sure if he had what it took to help protect Hannah from a frightening disease.

After this discussion with Jeanne, Carl had a fitful night's sleep. At two o' clock in the morning, he was still tossing and turning. When he finally drifted off, he had a vivid dream. He had huge, beautiful wings, like an eagle, and he was convinced he could fly. He started to flap them, soon working them as hard as he could, but no matter how hard he tried, he could not rise more than a few inches off the ground. He was determined and tried again and again to lift off. He was exhausted but kept trying.

At one point in his dream, Carl finally gave up and decided he couldn't fly after all. Suddenly, out of nowhere, Jeanne and Hannah appeared. They also had wings. "They walked up and we all linked arms together, and somehow, we just took right off!" Carl remembered. "We soared through the sky. I remember thinking how effortless it was when we did it together, and how I could hardly budge when I tried it alone."

A Family That Flies Together, Stays Together

Carl's dream remained with him for days and weeks afterward. While he was driving to work or standing in line at the bank, his mind would drift back to the image of the three of them flying together. Every time he thought of the image, he felt a strong and persistent urge to be home, to be physically close to Jeanne and Hannah. His whole body was infused with energy, and his thoughts took on a new level of clarity—he wanted to open himself to the love Jeanne and Hannah had to offer. He knew definitively that he had found his new vision.

Carl's dream continued to inspire him to become more involved in family life. Hannah would look into the stands at soccer games and see her dad giving her a thumbs-up. The tending and weeding of the garden became an affair for all three of them. He even started leaving the school building at the same time as his colleagues. Fortunately for Hannah, Carl's second vision came in time to restore the bonds that may well have saved her from an eating disorder.

Carl was lucky—he'd had decades of experience with the energy and purpose a vision can bring. When that one ceased to work

for him, he knew instinctively that it was time to do the work to find another one. The six questions helped him open his mind to what his heart already knew—he was worthy of love. Asking himself **Who loves me?** helped him realize just how close that love had been all along.

Both Carl and Eileen, whom you will read about next, had a tough mile to walk before they could overcome their abusive childhoods. But while Carl had built a steady foundation of self-esteem based on his worth to others, Eileen had managed to insulate herself from others altogether.

EILEEN: GIVING YOURSELF TO LOVE

Eileen's adoptive parents forgot her birthday not once, but twice. Still, if their transgressions had been limited to a few occasions of simple forgetfulness, perhaps Eileen would've had a different story to tell.

Her parents were very rigid and distant emotionally, but vigilant—bordering on obsessive—about her biological functions. Even when she was too full to eat, young Eileen would be forced to sit at the dinner table for hours, choking down cold vegetables and boiled meat. Her parents believed in home remedies, but the cure for every illness seemed to be forcefully administered enemas, to which Eileen had to submit even when they just *suspected* she was sick. Understandably, Eileen developed a well-honed ability to conceal her colds and sicknesses, a trait she carried into her adulthood.

Eileen spent most of her childhood time in a secret hiding place in her attic, a protected haven where she kept her collection of toys and stuffed animals, books, and a pillow and blanket, all hidden in cardboard boxes. Over time, she also managed to spirit away some pieces of lumber from her father's workshop and used these to build a makeshift floor, about six feet square, next to the attic vent where, except on the coldest winter days, she could curl up and enjoy some light and fresh air. In this secret place, she would hide from the world and her parents, and for the only time in her life, she felt safe.

Although she was a good student with several friends at school, Eileen never brought anyone home—she didn't want anyone to meet her parents or see their home. Her shame only increased when, at age fourteen, Eileen was raped by an eighteen-year-old boy she'd had a crush on. She never said a word about it to anyone, keeping that secret inside for decades. When I asked her to describe herself as a child and teenager, she needed only a single word: invisible.

Eileen's first vision for her life came in an unlikely package. When she was twenty, she became pregnant by a man she'd had sex with exactly once. Although she ended the relationship, she decided to keep the pregnancy, and her plan for the future fell into place.

Eileen's decision to follow through and give birth to her daughter, Vicky, was the result of a formative vision similar to Carl's. The idea of becoming a mother became an organizing focus for Eileen's life. Until then, Eileen had been drifting, with no goals or focal point. Far from being scared, Eileen said that she found the idea of being pregnant comforting and energizing from the moment she got the results of the pregnancy test.

Vicky was now a twelve-year-old who'd spent the last year steadily shedding the vestiges of her girlhood body and metamorphosing into a beautiful young lady. She was starting to attract attention, which made Eileen nervous—a completely understandable reaction, given her own history with men. But the final blow came when she heard of a friend's adolescent daughter who'd recently been diagnosed with diabetes.

"When I first learned about her," she said, "all I could think was that I could never survive if something ever happened to Vicky. I have to confess, the thought had occurred to me that if I lost her, I'd probably just kill myself." A chill ran down my spine as I heard these words; the tone of her voice told me that I should believe her.

To say that Eileen's adult relationships with men had been disappointing would be a gross understatement. She knew the pattern well: Initially, she would be attracted to men who were superficially glib and outgoing, but on a deeper level tended to be self-centered, possessive, and rather needy. Some had even been abusive, especially verbally. "I'm like a moth drawn to the flame," she said, adding with a wry smile that she'd gotten "burned" more times than she could count.

Eileen knew that there was a better way, and in trying to build a better life for herself, she'd invested considerable time and money in reading about psychological wellness and going to personal counseling. She'd told me that she'd once been diagnosed with *borderline personality disorder*. Even the name depressed her. "The books said that means I have a problem with 'boundaries' with men," she said. "First I give too much, then I get angry, and finally I run away.

"Some of that is true—I can be very affectionate, but when I feel taken advantage of, I leave. But what doesn't fit is the idea that I lose my identity in relationships. The truth is, there's a part of me that no man has ever really touched," she said sadly.

Second Vision

After living her life according to the vision that had guided her from the moment of Vicky's conception, Eileen was forced to confront the idea that she'd come to the end of that path. Her first epiphany had carried Eileen far, but it was no longer enough to steer her into the future. What Eileen needed now was a new organizing vision for her life.

The impetus behind this need was the healthy realization that her life was about to change dramatically. Like it or not, Vicky's impending departure from childhood meant that Eileen had some new choices to make. She understood that she could not continue to be attached only to her daughter. It was tempting, but wrong for both of them. It was time to start letting go, so that her daughter could grow and develop her own identity.

The question *Who loves me?* became a pivotal one for Eileen. In looking at her relationships through this lens, Eileen came to see that she'd actually dated a few men who were different from her usual choices, men who weren't immature, self-centered, or abusive. "They actually wanted to love me, I think." She smiled. "But, of course, I dropped them right away! I remember thinking once that I must be crazy—I'm never attracted to normal men, only to egotistical sleazeballs."

We both laughed, but actually this comment made a lot of sense to me, especially in light of this theme of being loved. To be loved, we must first be open to it. By gravitating toward self-centered and immature men, Eileen was protecting her heart. She knew instinctively that those men weren't ready or able to love someone else.

The Breakthrough in the Book

Breakthroughs often come at the most unexpected times and in the most unexpected ways. It is not possible to predict exactly which questions (or combination of questions) will trigger a vision, or when it will happen. For Eileen, the fateful moment came one afternoon when she was helping Vicky clean out her bedroom so they could transform it from a child's room to a young woman's.

As they sat next to each other on the floor of Vicky's bedroom, sifting through stacks of old storybooks, Eileen was reminded of their nightly ritual of reading together before Vicky drifted off to sleep. They'd cuddle up in Vicky's bed with a story of her choosing. This nightly ritual was a special time that would always be one of Eileen's warmest memories of motherhood. Now, though, it was time to store Vicky's extensive collection of books in some waterproof boxes for safekeeping.

They were about halfway through the stack of books when Vicky sat back against her bed, smiled at her mother, and suggested that they take a break and read each other a story. "I've never read to you, Mom," Vicky said. "Let's do it now, before we put these all away and forget about them."

Eileen was delighted for such a fitting celebration of their times together. First, she chose a book at random from the pile in front of her, and they sat close together on the carpet, leaning against Vicky's bed, as Eileen read.

When it was Vicky's turn, instead of choosing a book at random, she took a few minutes to survey the pile. Vicky smiled when she spotted a favorite, one that had been gathering dust on her bookcase for the past few years. The book was *The Velveteen Rabbit.*

As Vicky read, Eileen found herself in an unusual position: Although she had read this classic children's story to her daughter countless times before, this was her first experience of listening to it. But when Vicky read the follow passage, Eileen was hit with what she later described to me as "emotional lightning."

In this scene, two children's stuffed toys—a hobbyhorse and a rabbit—are talking to one another when they are alone.

> "What is *real?*" asked the Rabbit one day, when they were lying side by side near the nursery fender, before Nana came to tidy the room. "Does it mean having things that buzz inside you and a stick-out handle?"
>
> "Real isn't how you are made," said the Skin Horse. "It's a thing that happens to you. When a child loves you for a long, long time, not just to play with, but *really* loves you, then you become real."
>
> "Does it hurt?" asked the Rabbit.
>
> "Sometimes," said the Skin Horse, for he was always truthful. "When you are real you don't mind being hurt."
>
> —from *The Velveteen Rabbit*, by Margery Williams

Eileen could recall reading this passage many times. "I've read it, but I don't recall ever really hearing it," she said. Perhaps it was a matter of timing—maybe Eileen hadn't been ready to hear it before, but now she was.

Whatever the reason, the result was as profound for her as Carl's flying dream had been for him. Eileen found herself rereading the story of the velveteen rabbit many times, especially this short passage, over the next few days. She couldn't get it out of her mind.

What had happened, of course, was that Eileen had found her new vision. "That little passage described me perfectly," she said. "The only relationship I've ever felt 'real' in has been my relationship with Vicky. And Vicky happens to be the only person whose love I've been really open to.

"That hasn't been the case with men—not at all," she said. "'Unreal,' not 'real,' is the way I'd describe how I've felt in all of my relationships."

Eileen suddenly understood that to be open to love was to be "real," something she'd never done in her intimate relationships. Being in a relationship with a man who could not give involved no emotional risk. The real risk was to give herself to love, but thus far she had only done that once—with Vicky.

Eileen's new vision for herself meant having to approach relationships with men from a new perspective—she had to stop presenting the Eileen she thought they would like, and start sharing the Eileen that was already, gloriously, very real. One of the many side benefits of discovering our visions is the huge wellspring of energy they uncover. In Eileen's case, she began to realize with tremendous relief how much less exhausting it was to just be herself.

When she started out in pursuit of this vision, neither of us had any idea whether she would ever find Mr. Right. But she knew, beyond a doubt, that the way she'd approached men up until then virtually guaranteed that she would not.

Storybook Ending

Two years later, I got a call from Eileen. Her search to fulfill her vision had indeed been successful. Three months earlier, she'd married a man she'd been dating exclusively for nearly a year. He was someone she had known through friends for several years— known, but avoided. He was ten years older than she, had been married once, briefly, in his twenties, and led what Eileen jokingly called a "seriously normal life." That life included a good job, long-standing friendships, and hobbies. "Tim is a completely normal man who loves me to death," she said. "He has an incredible amount of energy, he's romantic, and he's thoughtful. Naturally, that combination made me want to run the other way!" We both laughed.

Tim's hope was that Eileen would consider adopting a child with him. A childhood illness had left him infertile, but he'd always dreamed of having a family. "I think he'd be a terrific father," Eileen said. She told me that they were on their way to adopting one, perhaps even two, children.

"One more thing," she said, before saying good-bye. "I feel very real these days, if you know what I mean."

OPENING UP TO LOVE

Visions can come in many forms, and they can catch us by surprise. Carl's vision came to him in a dream; Eileen's came in a simple passage from a children's book. The message in both cases was the same. These two people had, for various reasons, closed themselves to love. For many years, other things in their lives—careers, achievement, parental duties—had sustained them and given their lives purpose and meaning. But there came a point when the things that had compensated for being open to love were not sufficient anymore. Their lives had stalled, and they knew it. At that point, they each needed a new vision to carry them forward.

Although we cannot simply force a vision into being, exploring the six questions can help prepare our minds and set the stage for a new awakening. Both Carl and Eileen did just that, and for both of them the question *Who loves me?* turned out to be the key that eventually led to quantum change. For many people, *Who loves me?* may be initially a scary question, but they soon realize that they have one, two, even several people who love them unconditionally. Here are some exercises that can help you target these people and further explore this issue of opening yourself up to love.

Love versus Achievement

As with all of the six questions, when we change lenses from *What am I worth?* to **Who loves me?** our perspective is drawn inward, forcing us to look to our closest relationships for the answer. Open your journal to a fresh left- and right-facing page. Do the first exercise below on the left page, and the second exercise on the right. Seeing them contrasted like that will help to underscore the very large differences between the questions *What am I worth?* and **Who loves me?**

- (On the left page) First, think about your self-esteem in terms of your *résumé*. List six *accomplishments*, outwardly apparent things you've done in your life that you feel most proud of. Leave space between the lines to fill in with details of challenges you faced, adversity you overcame, and lasting benefits you continue to reap.

Now, how close is this résumé to your current self-image? What kinds of accomplishments have you included—your career? Your schooling? Your possessions or portfolio? Circle the words that best describe the traits that earned you those accomplishments.

- (On the right page) Next, list the *six relationships* you're most proud of. Note any challenges that you've overcome together, or any growth you've experienced as a result of that relationship. Describe how you feel when you spend time with that person, and briefly summarize yourself as you think that person sees you.

As you were writing these names and their corresponding challenges, how did you feel? Many people report that this exercise taps into a well of emotion they didn't realize existed. Did you feel a similar wave of sentiment when you listed your résumé? What does this tell you about the importance of this shift of lenses? Now, circle the words above that you'd most like to feel *all the time*. Often the people who love us most can see us best. You could be circling the very essence of *you*. Keep these words in mind as you answer all six questions in the next chapter.

Being Loved, Past and Present

Flip back in your journal to your attachment inventory from the chapter "Whom Do I Love?" Copy the list of people you were attached to as a child into the next page of your journal. For each person, ask yourself the following questions:

- Close your eyes and imagine this person's face, and envision him or her completing this sentence: "To me, you are. . . ."

- How did he/she express love? (Be as specific as you can in identifying the things that each of these people did that made you feel loved by them.)

- Did this person truly love you for *you*? What was the message you learned about yourself from that experience?

- Did this person withhold love, abandon you, or treat you cruelly? What was the lesson you learned about yourself from that experience?

People who have closed the door to love in self-defense, as Carl and Eileen did, can often get by for a long time if they have something else in their lives to compensate for their loss. Carl's sustaining vision was the pursuit of independence. Eileen's sustaining vision was motherhood.

Once we have closed the door to love, it becomes that much easier to measure our self-esteem in terms of our worth to others and society, and our culture only reinforces this kind of self-evaluation. But anyone who has felt unconditional love—and we all can, if we're open enough to recognize and accept it—understands that it blows any résumé *out of the water.*

Write an Ode to Love

There are those among us who fear the experience of heights, or deep water, or dense woods; for those who have shielded their hearts, like Carl and Eileen, the experience of opening themselves up to being loved is about the scariest thing they can imagine. It can take a lot of courage to face this deep, instinctual fear, but the benefits far, far outweigh the risks.

One exercise that can help when taking the first step toward confronting that fear is to write about how it feels to be loved. Unlike a love poem, which is directed at someone we love, the subject here is the sensation of receiving love.

Rather than get bogged down in the rules of writing poetry, think of your ode as the distillation of experience. It doesn't have to rhyme, it doesn't have to follow any form at all. Just use uncomplicated, clear words that express what you feel in your heart.

Try listing a bunch of emotions or images you associate with being loved, or recall a time or place where you felt loved, and try to recapture the smell, touch, and taste of that moment. How would a child draw that feeling? Write these details down in your journal.

Here is an example from the story of the velveteen rabbit that inspired Eileen's vision. In this passage, the Skin Horse is talking about becoming "real"—in other words, being loved.

> "It doesn't happen all at once," said the Skin Horse. "You become. It takes a long time. That's why it doesn't often happen to people who break easily, or have sharp edges, or who have to be carefully kept. Generally, by the time you are Real, most of your hair has been loved off, and your eyes drop out and you get loose in the joints and very shabby. But these things don't matter at all, because once you are Real you can't be ugly, except to people who don't understand."

Seek Support

The last line of the above passage alludes to a bitter truth about the world: There are people who understand what it means to be open to love, and there are also those who don't. Eileen made a habit of picking just the latter type of men. When you're reflecting on this theme and asking **Who loves me?** it's important to avoid the latter and to gravitate toward the former as much as possible.

Look around you. Are there people you know who impress you as being loved? Do they seem "real" to you, or better still, do you feel like you can be "real" when you're with them? Increase the amount of time you spend with these people, in any way you can. They are your best support system.

Conversely, is there anyone out there who you sense isn't open to love? People around whom you feel guarded or uneasy, or like you have to put on an act or impress? Do your best to minimize the time you spend around these people. They may need to shift their own lenses, but there's no sense wasting your time with them—or derailing your own vision—until they do.

You've taken time to consider the first five questions—the soil is very fertile for your vision. Until your path reveals itself, however, you need to gather the strength to stick with the lessons you've already learned, to stay open and ready for quantum change. That's where the sixth question—***How can I be true to myself?***—comes in, to sustain and inspire you.

SIXTH QUESTION:

How Can I Be True to Myself?

vs.

How Can I Gain Approval?

M. K.'S CHOICE CHANGED
HUMAN HISTORY

When Queen Victoria was declared the empress of India in 1877, the painfully shy and skinny M. K. was only eight years old. He was a typical boy, who stumbled over his math problems, spun tops, and played cricket. Though he sometimes stole money from his family's servants to buy cigarettes, the thought of lying soon filled him with disgust. He resolved that he would always tell the truth.

Although M. K.'s family wasn't very rich, his father still tried to project an air of wealth, keeping three different homes and wearing gold jewelry as a status symbol. M. K. was expected to follow in his dad's footsteps, so as soon as he was nineteen, he was sent to London to study law. He tried to please his parents and struggled mightily to fit in with the culture. Shivering in the cold, he assembled a Londoner's wardrobe and struggled to get his hair under control every morning. He took French lessons, elocution lessons, violin lessons, dance lessons. He even tried to eat meat, though it offended his Hindu beliefs.

He was a man caught between two conflicting cultures, trying to please both.

M. K.'s first post after finishing school was with an Indian law firm in South Africa. He became outraged when he was detained and questioned riding the train in first class with a legitimately purchased ticket. Initially, he took up the fight of any "properly dressed" Indian man's right to ride in first class, until he realized the more horrifying, widespread truth of discrimination against the indentured working class. In that moment, he found his purpose—to aid and support those with the least power.

M. K.'s training in courtroom tactics led him to approach each of his cases as a fighter seeking retribution, a role in which he never felt comfortable. One day, he decided to try settling a worker's suit with calm negotiation instead, and a deep sense of peace filled him. With this new philosophy of nonviolent protest, he had found a way to be true to himself. That small moment of insight would grow into a vision that would one day help M. K., later known as Mahatma Gandhi, free his country from the tyranny of English rule.

How Can I Be
True to Myself?

In times of personal and national turmoil, we talk about heroes and courage and the battle between good and evil. We hear about people with "character," but what does that really mean? We may think people with character have strong or forceful personalities, that they fight for what they believe in, that they're morally upstanding. When it's seen in this light, we may come to believe that character is the exclusive domain of firefighters or clergypeople or soldiers or peace protesters.

But perhaps character is not something found only in extraordinary feats of daring or selflessness; perhaps it is best reflected in the everyday choices we make about how we live our lives. Pioneering American psychologist William James described character as something very similar to the goal of the six questions.

> I have often thought that the best way to define a man's character would be to seek out the particular mental or moral attitude in which, when it came upon him, he felt himself most deeply and

intensely active and alive. At such moments there
is a voice inside which speaks and says: "This is
the real me!"

—from *The Letters of William James*, in a letter to his wife,

Alice Gibbons James, 1878

All of us are, in our souls, capable of being men and women
of character. Character is not a fixed quality—it's more like the
rules of the road, the recipe for being, the pathway of decisions and
choices that leads you through life. When we have character, those
decisions and choices are based squarely in the intention to honor
our truest purpose, no matter how we define it—and that's the key.
We have to define it.

We aren't born with character—we have to work on it, to develop it like we would a strong pitching arm or an eye for great art.
Character is what we earn when we finally learn that we *can't* always please everyone and still remain true to ourselves. Before we
can cultivate character, we have to break our addiction to *approval.*

As babies and young children, we thirst for affection and approval like water. The effects of love and attention on the human
psyche are obvious to anyone who's ever watched a child being
praised. Just as small children bask in the glow of approval, they
instinctively recoil from disapproval and anger. A scolding voice
can elicit cries from an infant who is still too young to draw any
connection between her own behavior and the disapproval it
evokes.

As we grow, the desire to seek approval, and avoid disapproval,
extends to include other significant people we admire in our lives,
such as coaches or mentors. We also learn that we're better off cul-
tivating the approval of other people, like teachers or bosses, not

for love, but as a means to an end—job security or good grades, a raise or a promotion. (Just think of how politicians make promises and hold babies—this approval-seeking is their stock-in-trade.)

Given this kind of an education, unless we've been actively encouraged to challenge the rules and stand up for our opinions, we will approach almost all situations by seeking an answer to the question *How can I gain approval?* It's not only the one most likely to grant the rewards of being good boys and girls, it's also the path of least resistance. Conformity is born of this question. The status quo is maintained by this question. But as when Robert Frost confronted those two roads that diverged in a wood, asking the question ***How can I be true to myself?*** and consciously choosing can make all the difference.

Think of ***How can I be true to myself?*** as the metaquestion of the six questions: It contains the essence of each question, yet we can only answer it when we have answered all the others. While *How can I gain approval?* can tempt us to make compromises that undermine our character, ***How can I be true to myself?*** strengthens our personal integrity with every choice we make for ourselves. ***How can I be true to myself?*** is our portable mantra, the all-in-one reminder of our identity, purpose, place, attachments, and worth. In any situation requiring a decision, no matter how small, when we answer this question honestly, we can act with confidence, knowing that we are doing the right thing. And what could be more freeing than that?

Both Karen and Curtis had struggled mightily with a lifelong need for approval. After working individually with each of the questions, it was the final question—***How can I be true to myself?***—that helped them synthesize all their learnings into one essential truth: their own visions.

KAREN'S STORY: IN SEARCH OF MR. MONEYBAGS

"My mother was a real looker, as they used to say," Karen told me. "Even now, well into her fifties, she still can turn heads."

A beautiful woman herself, Karen was just starting to realize how much her mother's beautiful exterior masked a cold and calculating heart. Karen's mother had been born into very modest circumstances that she'd been desperately running from ever since. Her parents worked as cleaning people in schools and private homes, but sadly, Karen didn't know much about them—those relationships were casualties left behind in Karen's mother's frantic escape.

What her mother lacked in education and background, she more than made up for in charm and sheer ambition. Her main goal in life was to find two rich men—one for herself and one for her daughter—who would provide them with security and luxury. She pursued her goal with ferocious determination. "I've still never met anyone as determined as my mother," Karen said, shaking her head.

Karen was born when her mother and father were both eighteen, but their marriage didn't last long. When Karen was four, her mom packed the two of them up and hired a mover to get them out of town before Karen's father or grandparents even knew they were gone. They moved to one of the wealthiest communities in a neighboring state, into a tiny apartment in a complex her mom had chosen carefully because it would make a good impression on the men Karen described as "her prey."

Within a year of moving, little Karen had lost all touch with her father and the rest of her family. Her mother spent the next decade on a methodical search for "Mr. Moneybags." "Mother never let any of the men she dated come to our apartment. She would stand by the window, dressed to the nines, watching for her date to pull up in his car," Karen recalled. "As soon as she'd spot him, she'd hurry down and meet him in the lobby."

On her days off, Karen's mom visited expensive stores, like Saks Fifth Avenue, with a measuring tape and a sketchbook in her purse. When she found something she liked, she'd take it into the dressing room, lay it out flat, and write down all the dimensions. "She knew places where you could buy nice fabric cheap, and she would make copies of these great dresses," Karen recalled. "I have to admit, I always had nice clothes, and no one ever suspected that they were homemade."

Somehow Karen's mom managed to work her way into the right social circles, usually by using Karen as a well-behaved prop. She joined all the right parent and community organizations and just so happened to chat up the decidedly rich women who conveniently also happened to have young children.

Without any of the family connections, the money, and the education that are usually the tickets into circles like that, her mother snuck in. She wormed her way into social invitations and cocktail parties, and soon she became a core member of every guest list. Her new friends were only too accommodating in introducing her to eligible men—after all, she had such style, such grace!

After several years that left a string of broken hearts in her wake, her mother eventually found a man who fit her criteria. He was rich and older, and she dug in fast. Once she'd landed her man, she never gave him a second thought. She now spent most of her time in New York, far away from her husband's home in Florida. "I don't believe she's ever loved him, not for one second," said Karen.

But now that she'd landed her own Mr. Moneybags, her mother's goal to pair up Karen took on the same fervor she'd once devoted to her own catch. "I was always my mother's backup plan," Karen explained. "She intended for me to marry a rich man, too, who could support both of us if necessary."

All the time Karen was growing up, her mother vigorously and relentlessly opposed any habits or ideas of Karen's that she saw as contrary to her own. "She could be truly overwhelming with what she called her 'opinions,'" Karen said. And her mother had "opinions" on just about everything—what Karen should wear, whom she should hang out with, where she should go, you name it. She could argue a point until sometimes Karen would give in just to get some relief.

When Karen did give in, her mother wouldn't indulge in a minute of gloating—instead, she'd turn around and shower her daughter with affection and praise. "Even when we weren't fighting, she'd tell me how gorgeous I was, how nice my hair looked, or how my figure was developing so nicely. She could tear me down, and she could also really build me up," Karen said.

Naturally, Karen wanted her mother's approval—and she always made it very clear how Karen could get it. That combination of intense disapproval and lavish approval was very difficult to stand up to. Of course, the approval and praise eventually extracted a huge price: Karen's sense of self.

Karen was forbidden to date until she was seventeen, and her first date was the senior prom. Her mother had arranged for a college sophomore to escort her. Karen's mother had high hopes for this pairing, because the boy's parents were very wealthy and he planned to go to medical school. As high as those hopes were, their relationship never really got off the ground—her date was more nervous than Karen was, probably dealing with the same kind of control issues with his own parents.

When graduation time rolled around, Karen's mother said she'd allow her to attend college if Karen lived at home and went to a school within commuting distance. By this time, Karen had begun to see that her mother's motives were less than selfless. "She just wanted to continue monitoring my behavior, which she did mightily," Karen said.

In spite of her mother's bullying, Karen managed to cultivate her own social life at college, and she even spent time with other young men while the matchmaking project went full steam ahead. Since her own ascension into the ranks of rich wives, her mother's access to the inner circles had improved significantly. Her mother actively scoured this cadre of wealthy friends to select prospects for Karen, and on a regular basis, she would tell Karen to expect a call from so-and-so, who was the son of the so-and-so's, about going on a date. She'd try to build him up with details that she thought Karen would care about, such as how much money his father made, how big their house was, or how much he stood to inherit when his old man died. She was oblivious to Karen's complete lack of interest.

Karen dated quite a few of the men she met this way, but continued seeing young men she met at college—much to her mother's consternation. It was around this time that Karen started fantasizing about transferring to a college far away. "I remember picturing myself living in a dormitory at a small college somewhere in New England. I was hanging out in my room with my girlfriends. I even had a boyfriend *I'd* chosen," she said.

This fantasy was no passing fancy—it may have been Karen's first vision. Sadly, while this vision represented an opportunity for

Karen, a door opening before her, for whatever reason, she decided not to pursue it at the time. "I couldn't—I had no resources of my own, and my mother flat-out refused to consider paying for me to go out of town," said Karen. Her only alternative would have been to finance her college education herself, on loans, a very unattractive concept to her at the time. It would be many years before Karen would realize that the risks may have been worth the benefits.

The Mating Game

By the time she was twenty-eight, Karen had been engaged twice, both times to men she'd met through her mother. The first one was her own age, an attorney on the fast track who was following in his prominent father's footsteps. The second man was more than ten years older than she, an investment banker, also from an established family. This "self-absorbed workaholic" (as she described him) would take long calls on his cell phone over dinner at a restaurant while she sat waiting for five minutes of his time. "Still, when he asked me to marry him, I said yes!" she said, incredulously.

Both times she'd been engaged, Karen could feel the relationship slipping away as soon as she got the ring. At that point, she'd tried to change herself in ways she thought would please her beau, keep his interest, and win his commitment, but this strategy never worked. Each time, the pattern was the same: The man would hedge and put off setting a wedding date, and months would pass. Karen would try to be patient, but eventually she'd want an answer. At that point, both men had opted out of the engagements. Karen could laugh about it now. "Both times, when I told Mother I'd given the rings back, she told me I should have sold them and bought some new clothes," she said.

Now thirty-two, Karen could easily see the connection between her mother's overbearing personality and her own tendency
to seek approval from men. Whenever she was with a man she
liked, whether it was a setup from her mom or someone she'd met
on her own, she would quickly lose herself in him. "When I think
of it now, it makes me shiver to think of how awful I felt if I sensed
my fiancé was unhappy with me for any reason, and the lengths I
would go to to get his approval," she said. With the benefit of a few
years, Karen could see that if she'd married either of these men, she
would have been following her mother's vision for her life, not her
own. "So maybe things really did work out for the best," she said.

BALANCING OUR NEED FOR APPROVAL

Whether the drive is conscious or unconscious, when we are
motivated to seek the approval of others (or to avoid their disapproval) too much, we risk losing any sense of ourselves as separate
individuals. Approval is a psychological lens that drives us *outward*—it forces us to depend on others to find out who we are and
where our lives ought to be going. That's exactly what had happened to Karen. She naturally wanted her mother's approval, and
her mother used this situation to control her daughter.

Karen's story is a good example of how the approval of others
can become a seductive and powerful force in our lives. If we fail
to balance it, it exerts a tremendous influence on the choices we
make. The desire for approval is even stronger for those of us who
were starved for affection and approval as children, or whose need
for love was systematically used to control them. In these kinds of
people, the need for approval becomes a constant hunger—a
never-ending quest to fill an emotional void.

Several famous entertainers, actors, and political and religious leaders have come from just this kind of background. Their unquenchable thirst for the approval and the love of others may be obvious from the outside, but they may be totally unaware of it themselves. They may see themselves simply as outgoing, friendly people, or even as altruistic. The true test of how dependent we are on the approval of others comes only when we are faced with a choice that runs the risk of making us unpopular.

Character is undermined not simply when we seek approval—because this is a natural impulse—but also when our outlooks become imbalanced and we limit ourselves to only seeking the answer to *How can I gain approval?*

As I mentioned before, ***How can I be true to myself?*** is the last of the six questions for one very compelling reason. In order to be true to ourselves, we must first know the "self" we seek to be faithful to. If that self has been a person whose identity has been determined by others, we will automatically continue looking to others to decide what course to follow—just like Karen did.

If you think about the people whom you admire most, one big reason you admire them probably has to do with their capacity to be true to themselves, despite external influences. Through their actions as well as their words, these people communicate that they have a firm sense of who they are and the direction of their lives, and they are willing to defend those things.

Considering how we can be true to ourselves, as opposed to how we can gain approval, once again shifts our focus *inward*, where it is less vulnerable to the changing winds of others' opinions and whims. It gives depth to our identities—and this depth is *character*.

Finding Her Vision

In spite of the unbearable pressure she faced from her mother, at one point Karen had decided to ask herself the right questions. She started at square one, with *Who am I?* and worked all the way through to the sixth question, *How can I be true to myself?* With such a constant, tremendous force in her life, this question was particularly pertinent. Karen needed to make the space not only to have her own vision, but to allow it to unfold the way she wanted it to, without outside influence. What she most needed now was a safe haven, a place where she could think out loud and talk with someone who was willing to let her discover her own path rather than choosing one for her.

Karen's second vision did not come to her all at once, full blown, in a flash—rather, it came to her in pieces. It began when she asked herself the question *Whom do I love?* and realized that she wanted to continue dating one particular man despite her mother's disapproval—end of discussion. Her resolution to act based on what she thought of the man, rather than what her mother thought, also showed a heightened strength of character.

"So long as I allowed my mother to make all the important decisions in my life, I couldn't have any integrity," she said. "Until now, I've let men do pretty much the same. No wonder they lost interest in me—I think they lost their respect for me first."

Karen decided that she also wanted to do some work in discovering her truest self and began asking *Who am I?* and *Why am I here?* What immediately came up was her acknowledgment that her lifestyle was not her own. Because she had been locked into the question *What do I desire?*—a question her mother fed by paying her rent and her bills and giving her an entire wardrobe—she never had the courage to face herself and ask *Why am I here?* But once

Karen realized that she had the power to release her mother's golden handcuffs, **Who am I?** became a lot easier to answer—she no longer had to live the question *Who should I be?* to get all the rewards of her mother's approval.

Part of the incentive for releasing herself was Mark, a fellow graphic designer at work whom she'd been dating for about a year. "He's very good at what he does, but graphic designers usually aren't rich—at least, neither of us is," she said. "He lives in a condo an hour away from work because he likes the open space, but between his mortgage, car payment, and gas bill, it's about all he can do to keep up."

Mark clearly didn't qualify as the rich guy Karen's mother had intended for her to marry, but she wanted to give her mother a chance to accept him. She wasn't sure how it would work out, but she knew beyond a doubt that **Whom do I love?** had steered her in the right direction—to Mark.

Asking New Questions

One evening, Karen's mother had started her usual game. She began by telling Karen how beautiful she looked, flattering her figure, and generally wearing down her defenses so she could start in like a fishmonger about the latest filthy-rich nephew of a friend. When Karen told her she was dating someone and wasn't interested in anyone new, her mother just ignored her words, as she always did, as if Karen hadn't spoken.

"She looked at her calendar and read off a few dates when this guy could come visit. I started putting my coat on to leave and told her I was going home," Karen recalled. "She glared at me and said, 'Don't tell me you're throwing away everything you have to offer on some graphic artist!'"

That last remark pushed Karen over the edge. She walked out and decided she would not speak to her mother until she had truly worked out the answer to *How can I be true to myself?*

Within days, her answering machine held several sweet-talking messages from her mother, but she decided not to return them. "I know how powerful she can be and I just don't want to take a chance of losing my resolve yet," Karen said. Being true to yourself can sometimes mean that you have to protect yourself through extreme measures. Dealing with disapproval had always been extremely difficult for Karen, so in this case, avoiding her mom gave her time to get stronger on her own.

The next weekend, Karen and Mark went for a long, rambling hike in the state park closest to his condo. They stopped to sit on the grassy bank beside a pond and watched a female duck paddle slowly back and forth with her four little ducklings in tow. "They looked so serene, and I just loved watching them," Karen said. "All of a sudden, I knew the answer to *Where do I belong?* I turned to Mark and told him that I was going to leave the city within a year and move somewhere where I could have access to a place like that pond—somewhere that I could go and take a long, quiet hike or sit and soak up that feeling of serenity."

Until that moment, it had never occurred to Karen that she really had a choice about where she could live, and holding fast to her own answer for *How can I be true to myself?* had made it possible. Mark laughed with joy and celebration for her enthusiasm, not in the mocking, controlling way her mother had. Over the next several months, Karen's relationship with Mark deepened. They planned to announce their engagement during Mark's birthday celebration with his family.

As for her mother, Karen said that she was protecting their secret until after their announcement—even then, she wasn't sure if she would invite her mother to the wedding. They planned to hold it in Maine, near Mark's family—and whether her mother's disapproving looks and condescension would be in attendance was still up for debate.

A Shared Vision

Karen's vision became the driving force behind what emerged as a shared vision for her and Mark's future together. They agreed that Portland, Maine, an hour from Mark's family, afforded them all the opportunities they had dreamed of: to live close to nature and open space, to buy a house of their own, and to find enriching work in their field. As is often the case with quantum change, a coincidence helped to spur them even further forward: Mark's cousin had recently started an advertising agency and was looking for a few good designers—and, eventually, partners. Buoyed by the strength of their resolve and their bond, the two took off for the great North and never looked back—thanks to Karen's vision by the pond.

CURTIS'S STORY: POET'S HEART

Like Karen, Curtis was an only child raised by a strong mother on her own, although his circumstances had nothing to do with social climbing.

From the day Curtis was born until he went away to an Ivy League college, he lived with his mother and two aunts in a big two-family house. Curtis's father had been in the Navy, but four months before he was scheduled to discharge, he had suffered an unfortunate accident. The resulting injuries left him with serious physical limitations, but his head injury was the worst. Despite a massive rehabilitation effort, his doctors were unable to reverse his rapidly advancing depression and personality change. Within a year after leaving the Navy, Curtis's father reentered the government hospital where he'd been treated, never to emerge again.

Over the years, Curtis visited his father on a fairly regular basis, but due to his father's limitations, the two couldn't have a particularly deep relationship. Meanwhile, Curtis found his niche in school—he loved to read and went on to earn a doctorate in literature from a respected university. Though his advisors had pressed him to seek an appointment at a major school, Curtis had opted for a position at a local two-year community college. He easily earned tenure and settled into a predictable, if somewhat less than challenging, routine. His colleagues held him in high regard, and he was often asked to participate on important institutional committees.

When I first met Curtis, he had recently separated from his wife, Kathleen. She'd shattered him with her proclamations. "She said she'd been living a lie for years and she couldn't go on that way," Curtis said. "She just didn't love me and thought of me more as a housemate than a husband."

Kathleen had been depressed lately, but Curtis never knew how to talk to her about it. Curtis confessed that their sex life had slid into nonexistence. But while he'd noticed that she'd become more irritable, he had no idea what she was thinking—and was too afraid to ask.

He took some consolation in the fact that she *didn't* say she'd never loved him, but that she'd stopped loving him. "She was turned off by my insecurity, my indecisiveness," said Curtis. "That's true—I do tend to second-guess myself a lot."

Around close friends and in the classroom, Curtis could be

self-confident, even a little cocky, and Kathleen had always been attracted to that side of him. But when they were alone or in unfamiliar situations, Curtis was different—he would vacillate over decisions and was tentative and fearful instead of adventurous and spontaneous. Kathleen had told him that she found these qualities irritating, but in the end, they even became repellent to her.

Beneath the veneer of self-confidence Curtis presented professionally, he tended to be painfully self-conscious. He admitted that he had sought Kathleen's approval and reassurance a lot, even over the most minor issues. A vicious cycle had set into their marriage—the more Curtis sought her approval and reassurance, the more testy Kathleen became, which only fanned the flames of his insecurity. On and on it went, as Kathleen's feelings for Curtis steadily deteriorated.

Curtis also sought approval from his colleagues and students. With these others, though, he'd managed to keep the true depth of his self-doubt secret. Many people thought of him as a wry and crusty person, one who couldn't care less what others thought. In truth, he was anything but that.

In private, Curtis fretted about his career—fretted, but didn't do anything. He worried that his lectures were dull. He worried that his colleagues secretly thought very little of him. Most importantly, he worried that he had set his sights too low, that he'd been underachieving by staying with his position at the community college. Yet at the same time, he feared that he couldn't possibly succeed anywhere else. "I chose to be a big fish in a little pond, though I'm not really comfortable with that," he said. "Kathleen was always encouraging me to move on. But as soon as I'd think about looking for a position in a university, or even a four-year college, I'd start to panic."

A Family Affair

Justifiably, Curtis's family was very proud of his accomplishments. "My family comes from a very modest background, so being a professor, even at a community college, is like being a Nobel laureate," he joked.

Perhaps even more important to his family was the stability of his position. "My mother and all of her sisters are champion worriers," he said. "Mom is the exact opposite of a risk taker. Even now, when I call her, she'll always ask me if I'm keeping up with my work, grading my papers on time, and so on. At least once every six months, it seems, she cautions me to be careful not to lose my job. I don't think she has any real idea of what tenure means."

More importantly, Curtis needed to figure out what tenure meant to him. Freedom from doubt, certainly, but a part of him also felt trapped. This is a common phenomenon—many people hold jobs they see as secure, yet are ambivalent about that very security. On one hand, they don't fear unemployment; on the other hand, they don't feel free to leave, even when they're unhappy. This was Curtis's quandary.

It was clear to him that his need for approval, and fear of disapproval, was becoming truly debilitating. As devoted a son and teacher as he was, Carl endured constant nagging doubts that he was good enough at either. While his real passion was writing poetry, he dared not share it with another soul. He would attend poetry slams and readings regularly, yet he hesitated to read a single piece of his own work in public.

Curtis was clearly a talented, sensitive, and kind man, but his life was foundering. What he needed was a vision that could jolt him out of his rut of self-doubt and his debilitating need for reassurance. As he began working with the six questions, I wondered what he might do with his vision when he found it. He would have to make a choice whether or not to pursue it, even if that meant taking a chance, including risking the disapproval of someone he loved. He would have to figure out his own answer to *How can I be true to myself?*

The Turning Point

As with Karen, a new relationship helped to create the turning point for Curtis. His vision began to unfold when he found himself attracted to one of his older students who was just a few years younger than he. Sharon was divorced and the mother of a six-year-old son. By day, she supported her son by working as an administrative assistant; by night, she studied and went to college to become a teacher.

Despite his interest, Curtis was very cautious around Sharon. The school's policy against intimate relationships between teachers and their students was extremely clear. Still, he found himself talking with her often, sometimes while walking together after class or stopping by the school cafeteria for coffee. Curtis felt no great urgency to cut these conversations short, and neither, it seemed, did Sharon. Toward the end of the semester, Sharon would even show up at his office door, bearing lattes, and they'd sit and talk for hours.

Curtis liked Sharon's sense of humor, and he admired the way she'd pulled her life together after her divorce. Since meeting her, his insecurity seemed to loosen up and lose some of its edge. "I find that I'm just myself with Sharon," he said. "Looking back, I realize how often I felt like I was walking on eggshells around Kathleen. I was looking for her approval. It's just not the case with

Sharon—I feel like she accepts me as I am." As fate would have it, while he was asking the question **Who loves me?** he stumbled on a highly promising candidate for the answer.

One of the biggest things that attracted Curtis to Sharon was watching her pursue her own vision for the future. Emboldened by his new answers, after the semester ended and grades were submitted, he took a risk: He called her at home and asked her out for dinner. After he asked, he quickly said he would understand if Sharon preferred not to see a faculty member socially. Of course, she had no such reservation—she was delighted.

Finding His Own Way

The two had been happily dating for a few months when Curtis took her to meet his mother and his aunts. The meeting was cordial, but Curtis could tell that despite his mother's smiles, something was wrong. He called her the next day to see what was up, and his suspicions were confirmed: She thought that Sharon was a beautiful woman, she said, but she wondered why Curtis would want to become involved with "an uneducated divorcée with a young child in tow." His mother's disapproval of the relationship presented a direct challenge to Curtis, a challenge he'd never before stood up to. This time was different—he had started to ask himself the question **How can I be true to myself?**

Every time he turned his back on his mother's or his own internal voice of doubt, Curtis became a little bit stronger. First, it was his admiration and respect for Sharon's courage in following her own vision that inspired him to submit some of his work to a poetry slam. When he'd asked himself **Who am I?** a voice came back very clear and strong—"a poet." For the first time ever, he read his work publicly, and the crowd responded well.

Not long after that, Curtis told Sharon about the idea of applying for positions at four-year colleges. Contrary to his earlier ways, he realized that he wasn't sharing these thoughts to get Sharon's approval or permission—he only wanted to let her see the idea that was taking form as his own vision. When he asked himself *Why am I here?* he knew that it was time to pursue his *purpose* in a more challenging arena. Moving in that direction would mean giving up his tenured position, but this idea didn't threaten him as much as it once had. On the other hand, he knew that when (and if) he told his mother, he would never hear the end of it.

He was willing to give up the security of his tenured position, but he didn't want to relocate—he felt that he already lived where he *belonged*. First, he loved his home. After the divorce, he'd bought out Kathleen's share of their house, which now reflected his interests and personality. His crowning joy was a series of extensive gardens of blooming perennials that he intentionally kept in a semiwild state.

The second reason Curtis didn't want to look that far afield was his relationship with Sharon and her son. Having asked himself both *Whom do I love?* and *Who loves me?* he knew that Sharon was the answer to both. Their relationship was energizing and brought out the best in him. With Sharon's son, Curtis had also discovered that he could love, and be loved by, a child. He looked forward to every opportunity to be with the boy and felt that they'd already established a close bond. Fortunately, there were several colleges and universities within reasonable driving distance, and he felt that he had a good shot if a position opened at any of these schools.

Curtis's vision was now complete, and it showed in his demeanor. Once he had answered all his questions, and he had a plan for how he could remain *true to himself,* he looked and acted like a free man. Having done the necessary investigative work, Curtis was well on his way to his own quantum change.

THE NEED FOR BALANCE

Our need for approval is natural—it's not something we should feel ashamed of, or embarrassed about. We all want others—especially those we love—to be proud of us. But if we sacrifice our integrity to our need for approval, it can become our Achilles' heel.

Neither of the mothers in these stories had evil intentions—to blame these women for their children's unhappiness would be unfair. Blame is not the issue. Each of us is blessed with the potential to lead a life that is guided by a personal vision. When we have the courage to be true to our visions, even if that means risking disapproval, we gain our own integrity.

In the end, when we take an inventory of our lives, we must answer only to ourselves. If the risk of disapproval seems intimidating, we shouldn't question the vision—perhaps we just need to spend more time with the sixth question and ponder the relative merits of *approval* versus *integrity.* When it comes down to it, which matters more? Would you want someone to be proud of you because you did what she wanted you to do? Or would it feel better to know that you earned someone's admiration, approval, and respect because you chose to be true to yourself?

Answering the Six Questions

If you have been doing the exercises in each chapter and thinking about the stories that have been told here, you probably have enough insight and ideas about your inner reality by now to begin drafting answers to each of the questions. Flip back over your answers to the exercises, paying close attention to the words you circled in each—are there any patterns? Do you see some words that come up very often? Be sure to address these core issues when you answer your very own set of six questions below.

If some questions still seem difficult to answer, go back and reread the chapter that focuses on that question, and give yourself a few days to reflect on it. Remember—these questions may seem simple, but they strike very close to our souls and may take some time, and courage, to answer. There is no need to hurry or pressure yourself. Your vision will be there when you are ready to uncover it.

Who Am I?

The answer to this question lies in discovering (or perhaps rediscovering) the talents, temperaments, and traits that make up our core personalities. Some of us may have lost touch with the people we are at our core as a consequence of powerful external influences, such as others' expectations for us. It is only after we have some sense of who we *are* that we can begin to assess whether the lifestyle we are living is really a good fit for us. Without this sense of who we are, we remain vulnerable to outside influences—to trying to be who others believe we *should* be. For example, is the real, inner you an introvert or an extrovert, spontaneous or playful, aggressive or compromising?

Who Are You? _____

_____

_____

_____

Why Am I Here?

It is possible for our journeys through life to be guided by two very different kinds of motivation. On one hand, we can be guided by continually asking ourselves *What do I want?* This outlook on life drives us outward, making us vulnerable to the influence of sophisticated marketing and advertising technologies. It also usually leaves us feeling only temporary satisfaction, for this question continually invites us to want what's new. A life devoted to the pursuit of what we want can easily turn us into careening pinballs, constantly changing direction under the influence of external forces. In contrast, when we seek an answer to **Why am I here?** we are moved to look within ourselves for the answer. We are more likely to discover there an answer—and a path—that can sustain us over time. What, do you sense, is your purpose for being here?

Why Are You Here? _____

_____

_____

_____

Where Do I Belong?

One way to define our place in the world is through the position we hold in some social, professional, or economic hierarchy. From this perspective, our sense of who we are becomes a matter of comparison, like first-class, second-class, or third-class passengers sailing on the ship of life. Viewed through this psychological lens, life is essentially a competitive process, one that renders us vulnerable to jealousy and envy. On the other hand, seeking to find an answer to **Where do I belong?** moves us away from defining ourselves and our place in the world exclusively through comparisons with others.

Whereas knowing our position may give us some sense of importance (particularly if that position is high in some hierarchy), it is no
substitute for the comfort and security that comes from knowing
what feels like home to us. Look around you, and answer the question: Is this where you belong? Where might "home" be for you?

Where Do You Belong? _____

_____

_____

_____

Whom Do I Love?

It is part of our human nature to become attached to *things.*
But if we allow this perspective to dominate our lives, we end up
defining ourselves exclusively in terms of our possessions. When
that happens, who we are becomes blurred with the question *What
do I own?* This kind of imbalance happens all too easily in our materialistic culture. To offset or balance this, and to create more balance in our lives, we need to look into our hearts for an answer to
the question **Whom do I love?** When we know that, we put ourselves in a better position to make choices that serve our best selves
instead of being influenced by an urge to preserve what we own.
The great stories of this world are full of examples of men and
women who chose love over property and possessions, and in
doing so found happiness.

Whom Do You Love? _____

_____

_____

_____

Who Loves Me?

In our society, it can be tempting to base our self-esteem entirely on our résumés. Most of us learn to ask ourselves *What am I worth?* to measure our value to others. But if we allow this view to become dominant, it leads to an identity built purely on a foundation of achievement and performance. Emotionally and spiritually, this approach can leave us feeling hollow and unfulfilled. To balance our self-esteem, we need to devote ourselves equally to being open to the love of others and to measuring our worth not only by our accomplishments, but in terms of who loves us and why.

Who Loves You? _____

_____

_____

_____

How Can I Be True to Myself?

The answers we've written to the questions above will dictate our success with the sixth question. Once we know the answers to the first five questions, we have the basis, the raw data we need to begin forming our visions. The sixth question draws upon our *character*, giving us the strength we need to stay true to ourselves, either in the face of disapproval from those we love or from our own self-doubts.

After working with the first five questions, many people find that the images of their "real" selves are starting to come together, but may be a bit sketchy at first. This is precisely when character is most needed—to protect the seed of that vision until it's strong enough to reveal itself. If we turn away from all that we've learned, we are only betraying ourselves. While it is natural to want reassurance and approval, the sixth question keeps us accountable to our own visions. Think about the traits and tendencies you've learned about—how can you recognize and avoid your own traps? How can you keep from derailing your own vision?

How Can You Be True to Yourself? _____

_____

_____

_____

All the tools we need to change our lives rest right here on these pages. Still, sometimes we want change so badly, we try to force a vision into existence. This pressure can be as counterproductive as fear and resistance to change are. Let's examine the ways we can best prepare for visions, quantum change, and "Living the Visionary Life."

Living the Visionary Life

Live all you can; it's a mistake not to. It doesn't so much matter what you do in particular, so long as you have your life. If you haven't had that what *have* you had? . . . What one loses one loses; make no mistake about that . . . The right time is *any* time that one is still so lucky as to have . . . Live!

—from *The Ambassadors*, by Henry James

In this closing chapter, we will examine several issues that you'll need to consider if you aim to lead a life guided by an inner vision, as opposed to one whose direction is determined largely by external forces like others' expectations. These hints can be helpful as you move forward into uncharted territory. We'll first look at how you can test and validate your vision in order to have the confidence that it is, in fact, a vision and not a mere whim. Second, we'll look at some suggestions for how you can get past frustrations and stumbling blocks to jump-start your quest for your new path. And last, but most importantly, we'll talk about how crucial it is to tackle your fears—the number-one foe of all visions.

PART 1: TESTING YOUR VISION

Let's begin by reviewing what a vision is, and what it is not. The ability to distinguish between a true visionary experience and sheer impulsiveness is essential—the former will lead to quantum change, while the latter just sets us up for disappointment and false starts. We'll also discuss how visionary change differs from simple escapism.

Visionary Change versus Impulsiveness

The worst fear that many have when asking themselves the six questions is that they will somehow mistake a momentary whim for a vision and then start down the wrong path, sacrificing too much and realizing their mistakes too late. What if Curtis's desire for a more challenging academic position had been a passing whim instead of a true vision? What if he had given up a secure job as a tenured faculty member in a community college only to discover that a new position as a junior faculty member in a four-year college was really not what he wanted and was no more satisfying than his current position?

Visionary change differs from sheer impulsiveness in many ways. First of all, visions are associated with very clear goals. Almost all of us know what it feels like to experience a whim, such as the sudden, fleeting urge to quit your job and live on a beach or leave your marriage and live alone. Such urges are easily understood as reactions to the burdens of adult responsibility, and they are usually the products of frustration. Even satisfying jobs, beautiful houses, and happy marriages can be burdensome at times; even fulfilling lives have their moments of frustration.

But we also know that simple impulses like the ones above tend to fade quickly. We pass someone on the street and find him or her attractive, or we see an ad for the newest SUV on television and want it. These are normal human experiences, and we know very well that these feelings will soon pass. Seeing a pretty face is not a message that we should abandon our families, rush up to the person we find attractive, and ask her to run away with us. Nor is a television ad a true image of the lives we should be leading (although the advertiser may hope we take it that way!). These moments of desire do not even come close to a cohesive view of the future or of the path we should follow.

Urges, impulses, and whims are part of our human nature, but some of us tend to experience them more than others. Impulsive people regularly have urges that come and go rather quickly. With these whimsical people, passing fancies quickly fade. Many impulsive people even know this about themselves, and they rarely have any difficulty distinguishing whims, which happen frequently, from visions, which are more rare. They can see whims for what they are—enjoyable daydreams—and leave them at that.

Persistence

One thing that separates a vision from a whim is its *persistence.* Whims come and go; visions, in contrast, linger and haunt us, even if we wish they would go away. A vision changes your view of yourself, your relationships, and your place in the world. All of the stories told in this book are testaments to the tenacity of true visions.

One way to test your vision, when you have one, is to see if it passes the critical test of time. If you've discovered a true vision for your life, you will find that it does not fade or lose its potency very easily. Even if you decide to set it aside—as many people do—you will find that when you turn to it again, it will be as compelling as it was when you first experienced it.

Visionary experiences are both energizing and comforting. Once you discover the vision within you, you will undoubtedly find that it quickly becomes not only a goal, but also something that can soothe you. It is like being lost in the woods and suddenly coming across a map that shows you the way home. Even if you decide to linger for a while in the woods, the darkness is no longer so terrifying.

Depth and Coherence

Other qualities that help separate a visionary experience from a whim are its *depth* and *coherence*. Whims and simple impulses are not only short lived, but also superficial. In contrast, a vision is more like a puzzle, composed of many interlocking pieces that suddenly come together, forming a seamless whole. Curtis's vision involved not only a romantic relationship, but also a bond with a child, a decision about work, a commitment to writing and sharing poetry, and a choice to remain in the same geographic area. His quantum change included changes on many levels.

Karen's vision was also multifaceted. Rooted in a strong desire to connect with the outdoors, she chose to work toward not only a new home, but also a committed relationship, a tougher stance with her mother, and an entirely new lifestyle. Her vision was a whole made up of interconnected parts.

In contrast to a true vision, a whim or impulse is typically much less coherent and organized. It is often little more than a vague thought—a "wouldn't it be nice if . . ." kind of experience. Whims don't come from the gut—they come from the head. They may entertain us, or amuse us, but they lack the power to really command and maintain our attention. A whim is only one piece of a puzzle, at best.

Compare your vision to some of the stories told here. If you are honest with yourself, it should not be difficult at all to separate a passing and superficial whim from a deep, lasting, and complex vision.

Invigorating and Clear

We have all heard others—and maybe we've done it ourselves—complain about being unhappy and talk vaguely about how they might change their lives. We may muse about looking for another job or wonder whether life would be more pleasant or fulfilling if we lived elsewhere. Although common, these experiences are not even remotely visionary. They fail to be truly energizing because they are fuzzy, vague, and often contain a hearty dollop of self-pity.

People are often discouraged from pursuing a true vision, even by their loved ones, because of their fear. They may say to themselves, "What if my so-called 'visionary experience' is merely a passing thought or an attempt to escape from an uncomfortable situation?" Visionary change, however, is significantly different from both escapism and vague, passing thoughts about a better life. When we experience visions, we are *energized*. All the restraints that have blocked us are lifted. The vision appears very clearly, like a doorway before us, pointing in a *definite direction* toward the lives we want to live.

Many people report that even long-standing feelings of depression are lifted following a visionary experience. And not only emotional balance and health but also physical health and vitality tend to improve as a consequence of quantum change. People can actually look physically different after discovering a vision—often years younger.

Visions versus Escapism

Having a visionary experience does not mean putting reality on hold. The sort of passing fancies mentioned above are usually totally detached from reality. When we indulge in vague thoughts of change, we don't think about the nuts and bolts of selling the house, relocating to a new area, or changing jobs—we just want it *now*. In contrast, when people discover true visions for their lives, they are typically very aware, from the outset, of all the pieces that make up those visions. They know full well that some of the changes involved could be daunting, requiring planning and persistence. Still, they are willing to embrace the effort required, because the vision they have chosen to pursue is compelling and energizing.

Escape is a very different matter. Escape is always associated with the feeling of relief, very different from being energized. A person may feel liberated if she decides to quit a job that has left her frustrated and unhappy for a long time. Similarly, people often feel some relief when they finally decide to end their bad marriages. While there's nothing wrong with feeling relieved under these circumstances, this relief is more a sign that you're leaving something bad behind than that you're moving on to something new and better.

When Karen and Curtis had their visions, they both experienced a renewed interest in life. Most importantly, their visions were associated with the clear goals and sense of direction that are the hallmarks of true visionary change. This is in stark contrast to decisions that reflect an escape from a bad or unhappy situation. When a person chooses escape over unhappiness, feelings of depression and unhappiness may linger alongside the relief. Many people experience this when they decide to break up unfulfilling long-term relationships—they find that the issues they associated with their significant others actually reside within themselves. You may recognize this phenomenon in the adage "Wherever you go, there you are."

Reevaluating a Vision

As we saw with Carl, the man whose childhood vision of independence carried him through to adulthood, sometimes a vision needs to be reevaluated. Instead of allowing yourself to get stuck in the same rut as Carl's, make it a habit to revisit your vision every six months to one year. Ask yourself these questions.

- Does my vision still touch me deeply?
- Does it still sustain me and give me energy?
- Does my purpose still seem clear?
- Do its pieces still fit together with an internal logic?
- Does it feel as real to me as the first day I conceived of it?
- Have I made progress toward my goals? Am I still fully engaged in quantum change?

If your vision no longer meets these criteria, it doesn't mean that the whole thing was a mistake—it just means that you need to ask yourself the six questions again, to make sure you're still honoring your truest, real self. As we grow, we may change in ways we could never have foreseen in our original visions. Remaining open to the possibility of continued growth and new perspectives is a key part of the sixth question, *How can I be true to myself?*

PART 2: FACILITATING VISIONARY EXPERIENCES

So you've read the six questions, thought about them, and done the exercises—and you still haven't had a vision. You may start to wonder, "Did I miss something somewhere along the way?

Is there another question I need to ask? Am I someone who just doesn't have a vision inside?"

The answer to all of these questions is *no*. There is no critical question you've failed to ask, and you most certainly are a person capable of having a visionary experience. We all crave visions to guide us, and we can become a little frustrated and impatient when they don't spring immediately to mind.

What follows are some simple, practical suggestions for things you can do to facilitate the process of discovering a personal vision. Some of these suggestions can help you to find answers to the six questions; others are intended to help you *stay out of your own way* so you can be open to the vision inside you.

Visions and Willpower

Compared with mistaking a whim or a desire to escape for a vision, trying to force a vision to appear is even more troublesome. Impatience can lead to impulsiveness, and when faced with frustration, we may decide a half-baked vision is better than no vision at all. Not so.

The six questions are indeed a guide to quantum change, but assuming that just reading this book will cause a vision to come immediately is more than a little unrealistic. On the flip side, trying to will yourself to have a vision is also apt to backfire, making it even less likely that a vision will appear.

Think about what it's like to drive on a foggy night. You know the frustrating feeling of not being able to see the road in front of you very clearly. You may even be tempted to turn on your bright lights, but remember what happens when you do that? The brighter light of your high beams gets reflected back more intensely than the light from your low beams, and visibility actually gets worse, not better. Trying to force a vision is very similar—it will most likely make your vision more elusive, not more accessible.

It is important to keep in mind that visionary experiences and quantum change are natural and common human experiences. Telling yourself this—every day if necessary—can be comforting. As long as you are patient, have faith that your vision will appear, and avoid trying to force the issue, it is likely that you'll eventually find what you are seeking.

Visionary Experience and Contemplation

Visions don't drop out of the sky—they emerge from within us. While a visionary experience may have a spiritual quality to it, it is not a religious occurrence or something that arises strictly from prayer or contemplation. Many people find meditation and other forms of contemplation useful for centering themselves, improving their concentration, and strengthening their connection with the eternal. These skills may help in having access to our vision, but they will not get us all the way there.

Within each of us, we hold a clear and deep sense of who we are, why we are here, where we belong, whom we love and are loved by, and most importantly, how we can stay true to ourselves. When that vision is obscured, we cannot bring it forth through sheer willpower or the concentration of deep contemplation—we reveal it by simply opening ourselves up. As the stories told here reveal, once we have done our work with the six questions, our visions often arise within the context of normal everyday experience. Most likely, when it happens, yours will come to you that way, too.

If we look back on the history of visionary experiences, we find that the most welcoming stage is set when we've provided three key conditions: We develop a *receptive mind* (as a result of exploring the six questions); we allow a *period of incubation* for those ideas to take hold; and we have a *trigger experience* that spurs our subconscious minds to produce the vision. Simply closing our eyes and gritting our teeth will never yield the fruit that this three-stage process will.

That said, a number of activities can ready your mind for a vision. A colleague once commented that many of her good ideas—not necessarily visionary ideas, but good ones—came to her when she was jogging. One reason for this could be that any repetitive physical activity, like walking, knitting, raking, swimming, or canoeing, tends to have the effect of clearing our minds. Runners commonly talk about the pleasant state of peaceful clarity that settles over them after they have run a few miles. Perhaps such activity makes our brains more receptive to visions on a physical level, or maybe our minds are just not as busy thinking about all sorts of extraneous issues. Breaking free from such *busy*-ness and routine thought patterns not only helps us tap into our inner creativity and imagination, it is also critical in helping us become open to our visions.

The Company You Keep

Many a vision has never been realized simply because the seeker allowed herself to be surrounded by people who were unsympathetic or judgmental. Visions can easily fall victim to the influence of others who don't believe in the possibility of living a visionary life or may even be threatened by it. These people may sincerely care about us, but they have their own reasons to react with anxiety or disapproval. They may try to discourage us by calling us dreamers. They may suggest that we are immature. And they may caution us about the hazards of giving up what we have.

Being around such people can suck the life right out of us. One woman told me that while she was working her way through the six questions, her best friend and her parents openly teased her and ridiculed the very idea of quantum change. I wondered why she'd bothered to share her pursuit with them, but she said it had never occurred to her *not* to share this with them. She'd naively expected them to be supportive, and she was dismayed and disappointed with the reaction she got.

Regrettably, this woman's friend and parents may have been threatened by her interest in a new vision for her life. They'd known that she'd felt stuck and unhappy for a long time, but they may have believed that somehow a vision could lure her away from them. Locked into their own fear of change, they may have truly believed that she'd be making a huge mistake to give up the lifestyle she had, regardless of her unhappiness.

This woman's experience was not at all unusual. In reality, friends, family, and partners often harbor fears that a loved one will leave them as the result of a vision, or that a vision might change the relationship dramatically. Let's look at a couple of things you can do to minimize the chances that others' attitudes and actions will sabotage your search for a vision before it even gets off the ground.

First, you must learn the wisdom of keeping your own counsel. Unless you have good reason to believe that other people, even loved ones, will be sympathetic to your quest, think carefully before sharing it with them. Could they possibly be threatened by your search? (Note: It doesn't matter if you think they should or should not be threatened; rather, do you believe they *could* be?) Most people fear change that they perceive as being forced on them. Could your own vision somehow be perceived this way? If so, what can you do to assure loved ones that your relationships with them will not be destroyed?

Keeping your search for a personal vision private is not lying, nor is the comfort factor with sharing it necessarily a litmus test of any relationship. We all have a right to some privacy, even in our closest relationships. If you are using this book as a guide to finding your vision, think seriously about keeping this process private and protected, rather than exposing yourself to active discouragement.

Second, avoid situations in which you find yourself having to defend your interest in visionary experiences and quantum change. Don't argue about it, and don't try to change anyone else's attitude. Think of your quest for a vision as something like a spiritual philosophy—you have a right to your beliefs, and there is no need to have to defend them, much less convert others to your way of thinking.

The third thing you can do is to actively seek out the company of like-minded people. These people may believe in the power of vision and the reality of quantum change, or they may be people who seem to be following a fulfilling path in life. As you pass through your daily activities, keep your eyes and ears open, and when you find people who seem particularly happy with the way their lives are going, gravitate toward them. Meanwhile, avoid those whose lives seem stuck and, more importantly, who act as if that's the best they can hope for.

As Henry David Thoreau once wrote, "The mass of men lead lives of quiet desperation," but you don't want to be one of them. Keep in mind how easily we can be influenced by the expectations and outlooks of others. I've met many people whose visions came to them quickly once they began associating with others who were pursuing their own visions or avoided people who were discouraging. If you are sincerely seeking a new path for your life but you're feeling frustrated, look to the company you keep.

Keep an Open Mind

Never be afraid of being called a dreamer. On the contrary, be proud of that label—it means that you have an open mind and can see things that others may not let themselves see. Indulge yourself in daydreaming, but remember—a vision is much more than a daydream. When you discover your own way, you'll realize just how much more.

Most of the people whose stories are told here experienced their visions when they least expected them, when their minds were open and wandering. Giving ourselves several moments during the day just to muse on the clouds or remember a pleasant event from the past can help us to overcome anxiety and open our minds.

While most had spent time asking themselves the six questions, the majority of people I've spoken with received their visions after a period of incubation that allowed those ideas and themes to gestate and bear fruit. In most cases, the vision also appeared in response to some stimulus: reading a book, looking at a photo, giving a talk, having a dream, and so on. While incubation often just takes time, here are some suggestions for how to open yourself to new stimuli that might just prove to be vital links to your vision.

Read biographies and memoirs. In particular, read about people who have lived visionary lives, but don't restrict your search to celebrity or explorer biographies. Look in the memoir section of the bookstore and keep in mind that ordinary people like you and me can lead visionary lives just as famous people have.

Try new and exciting activities. As a rule, rigidity is the enemy of visionary change. If you want to open yourself to a vision, make a habit of looking through your local newspaper's arts and entertainment section. Commit to attending at least one activity in your community each month—you'll naturally gravitate toward those activities that appeal to you, and each of those events will be filled with like-minded people.

Visit a new place every month. A day trip to a neighboring town, a peek into a new library or museum, any place you've never been before can help expand your horizons. Many people think of travel as an expensive, elaborate process that takes you far from home, but it doesn't have to be. One woman even took a trek to the Himalayas after she got divorced, hoping to find a vision for the rest of her life on a mountaintop there. Although her trip was memorable, her vision eluded her, and I couldn't help thinking that she was trying to will her vision into existence instead of remaining open and receptive. Interestingly, when this woman did find her vision, it came to her while she was quietly canoeing on a local lake on a crisp autumn morning, thinking of nothing in particular.

Meet new people. I'm not saying that visions can be found in the singles section of the newspaper. What I'm talking about here is something simpler—when you choose an activity that piques your interest, promise yourself you will talk, even briefly, with one or two people you meet there. Those connections can build bridges to your future.

PART 3: TACKLING YOUR FEARS

Quantum change, much like dancing, can cause some people discomfort. Not everyone who has a vision chooses to follow it. Some people even resist the idea of trying on a different set of psychological lenses and asking themselves the six questions. These people claim to not *want* to have a vision, just like some don't want to dance.

But in my view, visionary experiences and quantum change are natural and spontaneous human experiences. I believe that most of us will experience at least one vision, if not more, in our lifetime, *if we are open to it.* Let's put it this way: I have never seen a young child who did not like to dance, but I've seen quite a few adults who won't let themselves be dragged onto a dance floor and even refuse to allow their feet to tap in tune to music. While we are all born with a natural ability to respond to rhythmic music, some people *choose* to suppress that natural instinct as they move from childhood to adulthood. The same is true, I believe, when it comes to having a visionary experience—to *not* have one, we must actively resist our human nature. We may do this for many reasons.

Vision versus Stability

We are all born with not just one, but two potentially opposing instincts. On one hand, we yearn for a vision for ourselves. We long to live a life of meaning and direction. Without a vision, we are left to simply mark time in the present, treading water as life passes us by or even turning our attention to the past. A vision adds vigor to a life than can otherwise easily become stale, inviting us to look ahead instead of back.

On the other hand, we have an equally natural desire for *stability.* We may crave meaning and direction, but we are also creatures of habit who feel secure when life is guided and bounded by established routines and rituals. We like to view the world as a consistent, stable, and predictable place. This desire for security and comfort, much like our natural interest in dancing, is very much evident in children, who like nothing better than routine and stability. To some degree, we carry this need within us throughout our lives. But by their nature, visions have the potential to shake the foundations of our lives and they can create a certain amount of instability. This may be one reason why some people will find the idea of discovering their visions unsettling.

(In)Voluntary Change

Another factor that can influence our attitudes toward quantum change is whether we experience this process as voluntary or not. We all tend to fear, resent, and resist change that we perceive as being *forced* upon us. Such force represents a loss of control and often triggers feelings of helplessness and anxiety. It's one reason, among others, why children and teens often act up when they're told that the family has to move. It's also the reason why many of us dig in our heels when managers force us to change the way we do our work without bothering to ask us for our opinion first.

Our natural resistance to relinquishing our power of choice may make us fearful of pursuing the ideas presented in this book. We may feel threatened by the thought that we would somehow be forced or obligated to change our lives. To calm such fears, remember that while the themes explored here have the power to stimulate a vision, the power of choice still resides within the individual. The choice of pursuing your vision, part of it, or none of it—or even postponing it until the timing is better—is always *yours*.

Internal Enemies

Another, and a more troubling reason why we may act as if we fear quantum change has to do with a lack of self-confidence.

Many people who are afraid to dance are highly self-conscious or insecure. The same forces may be at work in those people who react the most negatively to the idea of quantum change. In words and actions, these people are saying, "I'm afraid of change! I want to stay as I am!" just like the person who says, "Leave me alone, I don't want to dance!" Sadly, these same people may have had a vision for themselves at one time (just as they probably liked to kick up their heels at one time), but may have lacked the confidence to pursue it. They often compensate for this by telling themselves and others that visionary change is a myth or a dangerous impulse that should be resisted at all costs. This is the way that fears of leading an enlightened life can be passed from one generation to another, just as low self-esteem can be.

Fear of Total Destruction

Last, but not least, there are those of us who will hesitate to open ourselves to these questions and explore these themes because we fear that a vision is something that will somehow take control of us and destroy our lives. History is filled with people who made dramatic visionary choices. Gandhi gave up a law career to pursue his vision of social justice. Paul Gauguin abandoned a career as a stockbroker to pursue his passion as a painter. Yet there are other examples that may scare us off, like Amelia Earhart, who studied medicine before she discovered her passion for flying, or Christa McAuliffe, who taught school before she became an astronaut and American hero. While they are inspirational for their willingness to dream and their courage to pursue their visions, tragically, both women lost their lives in pursuit of their visions. Admittedly, these kinds of stories can be unsettling.

Though we may not believe our visions have the capacity to actually kill us, many of us act as though finding a vision for ourselves would mean the destruction of our lives as we know them. But what we fail to appreciate is the level of control each of us has over the execution of our visions. True, a vision may compel us to move in a different direction, based on a change in perspective, priorities, or values, but a vision does not *force* us to do that. For every Gauguin or Earhart, there are thousands who pursue their visions without turning their lives upside down.

Instead of waiting and worrying and wondering what could be, you have to simply *go for it*. Don't let the "what ifs?" trap you. Make a rule that every time you ask, "What if the worst thing happened?" you also have to ask yourself, "What if I felt no fear?"

Your Vision in the Present

One last objection that people sometimes voice is, "But visions are all about the future. What if I don't want to look into the future? What if I want to live in the present?"

The reality is, when we close the door to a vision, we are not living in the present—we are always stuck in the past. The refusal to move forward in our lives usually points to our stubborn refusal to reevaluate something we learned long ago, whether from our parents, our experiences, or our lack of faith in our own ability to grow.

The people who have truly learned to live in the present are living their visions every second: They know who they are, why they are here, where they belong. Most likely they have no need to prove their worth to others or to surround themselves with material possessions. They have found a path that not only allows them to be true to themselves, it encourages this on a second-by-second basis. People who genuinely live in the present are actually the embodiment of *completed* quantum change.

Once we fully realize that our problems lie within us—perhaps related to our personal histories, but nevertheless in *ourselves*—then we are truly free. At that point, continuing to stay fixated on the past loses its value. Continually raking over your past in the hope that it will reveal the road to happiness is usually little more than a dead end.

Although many forces may conspire to discourage us from seeking or following our visions, casting blame on things that cannot be changed will just get us stuck. We need to let go of the past in order to move toward the future.

Fear of Change

Take some time to honestly confront any fears you may have about quantum change. They're not unusual—it would be more unusual for a person *not* to have any anxieties or concerns about this kind of change. Most of us, after all, have committed to some course in life. We may not feel totally satisfied or fulfilled with that course, but at least we are familiar with it. Quantum change definitely represents a challenge to the inertia that can take over our lives. Charting a new course can energize us, but it can also frighten us. Acknowledging any fears you may have will allow you to be more honest and help open your mind as you work through the six questions.

I hope these stories and suggestions will be a source of comfort, guidance, and encouragement as you embark on your quest to discover your vision. Ultimately, visionary experiences and quantum change represent challenges of faith—faith in ourselves.

It is only by risking our persons from one hour to another that we live at all. And often enough our faith
beforehand in an uncertified result is the only thing
that makes the result come true.

—from *The Will to Believe,* by William James

For your vision to have any power, you must have the courage to feel the fear, but *do it anyway.* Every man and woman you've read about has faced that fear. Their faith fortified them to ask the six questions and answer truthfully, to have patience until their visions revealed themselves, and most importantly, to walk through the doors that had been revealed to them. This decision, to follow your vision, is always *your* choice. On the other side of the threshold, your new life awaits you.

POSTSCRIPT

Having outlined here the theory of quantum change and shared many stories of people who found their visions, I am interested in hearing from you. Stories, comments, and questions are welcomed and can be sent to me at the following e-mail address: jnowinski@earthlink.net.

Although I cannot guarantee a response to every message sent, please be assured that I value your message and will read it with great interest.